What if you really could turn things around in your relationship? Things like anger to understanding? Frustration to fulfillment? Clear communication instead of misunderstanding? Or conflict to the closeness you've always wanted? I know Dr. Mitch Temple well, and I also know that what he shares in this outstanding book can help you begin to do just that in your relationship—starting right now! Pick up the book!

John Trent, PhD
Author of *The 2-Degree Difference* and president of
The Center for Strong Families

Mitch is the kind of leader you can trust. His advice on how to turn around a marriage is solid and is vital for couples in the world we live in. Don't settle for "just getting by" or the status quo in your marriage when you can have something so much better—and soon! We highly recommend *The Marriage Turnaround* for all couples because you never know when you might need it or someone you love might need it too.

Pam and Bill Farrell
Bestselling authors of *Men Are Like Waffles,*
Women Are Like Spaghetti

Some of the major barriers to having a great marriage are the many unrealistic expectations and "myths" that couples bring into their marriage. In this encouraging book Mitch not only explodes the unhelpful myths but he gives couples simple and practical ways to turn a mediocre marriage into one that is thriving and healthy. This isn't just mere theory. It's practical wisdom that you'll be able to immediately apply to your own marriage.

Gary J. Oliver, PhD
Author of *Mad About Us: Moving from Anger to Intimacy with*
***Your Spouse* and executive director of The Center for**
Relationship Enrichment at John Brown University

D1014354

If a marriage is in trouble, it is because someone is operating on bad information. Mitch Temple not only identifies the problems, but shows you how to re-program your mental and spiritual computer. Every married couple will find help in *The Marriage Turnaround.*

> **Gary Chapman, PhD**
> **Author of *The Five Love Languages and Love as a Way of Life***

This book connects with one of my passions about marriage—the heart! When your heart is out of whack, your entire marriage will be too. Mitch explains for us so clearly that "if you don't address the heart, the very thing that drives negative emotion and behavior in a relationship, your marriage will not be what you hoped for." I highly recommend this book for every Christian couple today. This book is male and female friendly! It guides you with practical, biblical, and humorous insights to lead you to the "turnaround" you have been looking for.

> **Gary Smalley**
> **Author, founder and president of the**
> **Smalley Relationship Center**

The Marriage Turnaround offers rich advice for any couple who longs to see their marriage dramatically changed into a great marriage. We were touched by the concept of becoming "ditchdiggers" by serving each other in marriage. We deeply appreciated the application from the Old Testament on how God answered the three kings' plea for help as they got down, got dirty, and used some backbone. How much more He delights *over us* as we get down off our high horse, take off our crowns, and fold each other's laundry on a daily basis! We loved it!

> **Dr. Gary and Barbara Rosberg**
> **America's Family Coaches**
> **Authors of *6 Secrets to a Lasting Love,* co-hosts of**
> ***Dr. Gary and Barb Rosberg—Your Marriage Coaches,***
> **and nationally known speakers**

THE MARRIAGE TURNAROUND

HOW THINKING DIFFERENTLY ABOUT YOUR RELATIONSHIP CAN CHANGE EVERYTHING

MITCH TEMPLE

MOODY PUBLISHERS

CHICAGO

All Scripture quotations, unless otherwise indicated, are taken from the *Holy Bible, New International Version®*. NIV®. Copyright © 1973, 1978, 1984 by International Bible Society. Used by permission of Zondervan. All rights reserved.

Scripture quotations marked NKJV are taken from the *New King James Version*. Copyright © 1982 by Thomas Nelson, Inc. Used by permission. All rights reserved.

Scripture quotations marked NLT are taken from the *Holy Bible, New Living Translation*, copyright © 1996. Used by permission of Tyndale House Publishers, Inc., Wheaton, Illinois 60189, U.S.A. All rights reserved.

Scripture quotations marked KJV are taken from the King James Version.

All websites listed herein are accurate at the time of publication, but may change in the future or cease to exist. The listing of website references and resources does not imply publisher endorsement of the site's entire contents. Groups, corporations, and organizations are listed for informational purposes, and listing does not imply publisher endorsement of their activities.

Editor: Afton Rorvik
Cover Design: Kirk DouPonce, Dog Eared Design
Interior Design: Ragont Design

Library of Congress Cataloging-in-Publication Data

Temple, Mitch, 1962-
The marriage turnaround : how thinking differently about your relationship can change everything / Mitch Temple.
     p. cm.
Includes bibliographical references.
ISBN 978-0-8024-5014-2
1. Marriage. 2. Couples--Psychology. I. Title.
HQ734.T273 2009
248.8'44--dc22

                                        2008032038

We hope you enjoy this book from Moody Publishers. Our goal is to provide high-quality, thought-provoking books and products that connect truth to your real needs and challenges. For more information on other books and products written and produced from a biblical perspective, go to www.moodypublishers.com or write to:

Moody Publishers
820 N. LaSalle Boulevard
Chicago, IL 60610

1 3 5 7 9 10 8 6 4 2

Printed in the United States of America

First and foremost, I would like to dedicate this book to Rhonda, my beautiful wife of twenty-six years, who continues to reign without equal. You are my partner, manager, advisor, mentor, and utmost admirer. You are the Creator's wonderful gift to me. Through your life, I've been allowed to experience a glimpse of divine unity and unconditional love.

Secondly, I would like to dedicate the spirit of this project to my only brother, Brad, whom the Lord called home January 14, 2005. Though his life was like a breath, his days were enormously rich with wisdom, depth, patience, compassion, and faith. I miss him dearly but know that we will ride together again as we did as young boys.

Contents

Preface

THE LORD HAS BLESSED ME WITH the honor of working with hundreds of couples, many just like you. I have seen the best of marriages and the worst. I have held couples in my arms as they moaned and wept because they didn't want to go on. And I have laughed and praised God with couples because they pulled their marriage out of the fire.

Many of the stories you will read in this book are true, although I have changed names and details to protect the privacy of the individuals. In some cases, the people you will read about are composites of those I have encountered through my years of counseling. In either case, I'm sure you'll be able to identify with many of the situations presented in these pages.

I don't want to make any promises that this book will be the miracle you are looking for to make your marriage a little stronger or turn it completely around. But my prayer is that you will find one or two principles or ideas that may work for you, now or down the road.

In this book, I want to help you identify ways you are thinking—about your spouse, about your marriage—that may very well be making your relationship more difficult than it needs to be. I want to help you build a stronger foundation for your marriage. My heart is to help you bring hopeful vision back into your marriage—to help you transform your thinking and turn your marriage around.

Believe me, it is possible.

Acknowledgments

THANKS TO DR. JOHN TRENT for his undying support, encouragement, and mentoring through this project.

Thanks to Dr. Gary Rosberg for his incredible friendship and encouragement to "keep writing" and to "guard my heart."

Thanks to Focus on the Family and Focus senior vice president Clark Miller, for allowing me to serve in the role of Director of Marriage. Also thanks for your prayers, your marketing, and your overall support of this project.

Thanks to Larry Weeden, one of the best in the business. Larry, I will never forget your support and direction on writing, publishing, and "voice" development.

Thanks to an old friend Cathryn Broadbooks, who believed in me enough to encourage me to "just start" writing many years ago.

Thanks to Dr. Peter Larson of Life Innovations for reading my material and keeping me on the clinical straight and narrow.

Thanks to Shanna Shutte, Afton Rorvik, Betsey Newenhuyse, and Larry Libby who edited, cut, and diced to make the manuscript sing.

Special thanks to Steve Lyon, Moody Publishers editor-in-chief, and his team for believing in this project and for making it easy to wade through the world of publishing a book.

Special thanks to Blythe Daniel, my Southern agent friend and coworker, who saw potential in this idea from the beginning and went beyond the call of duty.

Special thanks to Mom and Dad for encouraging me to be creative and for the "you can do it" attitude.

Introduction

LET'S START BY HAVING A LITTLE FUN.

No doubt you've heard people talk about "urban legends." These are stories—not necessarily urban—that get repeated again and again until many people begin to swear by their accuracy and veracity. Then, when someone comes along with the inconvenient facts to expose these apocryphal tales as a hoax or a myth (or at least a gross exaggeration), many have a difficult time letting go of the stories.

"How could it be a myth? I've read that a thousand times. It has to be true."

People used to speak of old wives' tales, conjuring up a picture of whispered gossip over the back fence. Today, the Internet is the biggest back fence that ever was, with cyber-whispers crisscrossing the entire planet in the blink of an eye. False stories get forwarded in chain e-mails from sincere people you know and love—or appear in authoritative-looking websites. *"It must be true—I read it off my computer."*

Even going beyond the realm of urban legends, many people have held certain assumptions for years—simple propositions that seem logical, plausible, credible . . . and are completely untrue.

For instance . . . you may have assumed that German chocolate cake originated in Germany. (Those Germans sure know their chocolate!) In fact, it was created in the 1850s in Dorchester, Massachusetts, using a chocolate bar developed for Baker's Chocolate Company by an Englishman named Sam German.

For that matter, India ink never came from India and Panama hats have nothing to do with Panama. (You already knew that no self-respecting Frenchman would claim a national origin for french fries.)

And did you happen to believe that mobile homes got their name because they began life on wheels? No. It's because they were originally created in Mobile, Alabama.

Are you ready to be shaken even further?

Eating turkey does not make a person drowsy, there are no alligators lurking in the sewers of New York City, you won't get cramps and drown if you go swimming less than an hour after you eat (sorry, Mom), poinsettia plants are not toxic, and lemmings do *not* commit suicide by hurling themselves off cliffs. Nor do you need to drink eight glasses of water a day.

Even the 1960s sitcom *Mr. Ed.* has been the subject of rumors and counterrumors. Several popular websites that claim to expose urban legends made the shocking disclosure that the talking horse wasn't even a horse at all, but a trained zebra painted up to look like a Palomino on black-and-white TV. (Zebras will move their lips but horses won't?)

Other websites were quick to debunk the debunkers. Mr. Ed was indeed a horse (of course, of course), and was made to look like a *talking* horse by feeding him peanut butter.

Some modern myths have become so entrenched in the popular psyche that no amount of authoritative, factual counterevidence can completely dislodge them. Consider the unfortunate case of the Procter & Gamble Company. Back in the 1980s the company received unwanted media publicity when an urban legend spread that their previous corporate logo was a satanic symbol, and that the company was somehow linked to the Church of Satan. With the rise of the personal computer and Internet, the rumor has been repeated and rehashed in countless forms. The company has no doubt spent millions trying to quell this whispering campaign, but eventually gave up and designed a new logo.

The secret to a marriage turnaround is "all in your mind," and I want to help you sort out fact from fiction in service of helping you build a great marriage. In the pages that follow, we'll consider some myths—some commonly held false assumptions—that aren't harmless at all. In fact, they can steal some of the most precious possessions to be found in this life . . . a peaceful home, a happy, intact family, and the lifelong friendship and companionship of a spouse who has seen you at your worst but still believes the best about you.

Chapter One

The Myths That Can
Make You Miserable

"The grass is greener on the other side . . .

until you get over there and realize it's artificial turf."

MY FAVORITE SHOW ON THE Discovery Channel, *MythBusters*, exposes common myths. Each week, the hosts, Adam Savage and Jamie Hyneman, challenge myths by using science to show the audience what's true . . . and what's bunk. Sometimes they even blow things up as part of their experimentation. What more can a guy ask for?

Myths that couples believe about marriage can be much harder to recognize than those on *MythBusters*. I'm convinced that marriage myths—false beliefs, unexamined assumptions—can make a couple miserable and mess up any good relationship.

I can't count the number of good-hearted, well-meaning Christian couples I've counseled over the years who've left their partner because of their belief that "I should be happy no matter what," or "I deserve to have an affair because of the way I've been treated," or the classic: "The grass is greener on the other side of the fence."

Here's a news bulletin: People on the other side, no matter how appealing they seem, are just as flawed as your spouse.

Maybe, like my wife and me, you strolled into marriage with more than a few crazy ideas about romantic love. Though Rhonda and I have enjoyed twenty-six years of matrimony, our success didn't come without struggle. We had to face down our own marriage myths soon after we walked the aisle.

I actually thought we would have sex every day, or at least every other day. Isn't that what every guy thinks? It took less than a week to put that particular myth to rest! One night I showered, shaved, slathered on my best cologne, and slid into bed, when I heard Rhonda practically snoring. Nothing like a little cold water to put my fire out.

Rhonda also brought her fair share of myths into marriage. She assumed, like many women, that I would always be as expressive and affectionate as I was while we were dating. Apparently, it didn't take me very long to fall short of that mark.

Both of our expectations were based on wrong thinking that brought emotional pain and some intense arguments into our young marriage.

God's heart breaks when He sees His children buy into myths and act on them. He grieves when He watches friends and family take sides and innocent children become emotionally wounded when they see Mommy and Daddy attack each other. God grieves when He sees the unhappiness, hopelessness, destruction, resentment, division, and financial strain that inevitably come when couples embrace marital myths.

Satan, however, is overjoyed.

THE ULTIMATE AUTHOR OF MARRIAGE MYTHS

If you had enough time, a detailed atlas, and some excellent hiking boots, you could trace every mighty river in the world back to its headwaters. Every river, every stream, every brook has its source. It comes from *somewhere*. It might flow from a deep, spring-fed lake, from a bubbling artesian well, or from some underground river that breaks free and flows down a mountainside.

In the same way, you can follow every lie, every deception, every false teaching, every harmful myth back to its headwaters. In fact, all of these things flow from the same source—Satan himself.

Jesus made that clear when He said of the Devil, "He was a murderer from the beginning, not holding to the truth, for there is no truth in him. When he lies, he speaks his native language, for he is a liar and the father of lies" (John 8:44).

Satan doesn't just have a casual disregard for the truth, he *hates* it. He began twisting, bending, and warping the truth of God's Word from the first words he uttered in the garden of Eden, speaking through a serpent.

If there is truth anywhere, Satan in his hatred will do everything within his power to distort it, dilute it, denounce it, or sprinkle it with just enough falsehood to destroy its intended meaning. Failing these tactics, he will seek to rip truthful words out of their proper context and drop them into a setting where they don't belong at all.

Every lie that was ever told calls Satan "daddy." Every false advertising claim, every instance of political double-speak, every used car salesman's exaggeration, and every "little lie" we utter can ultimately be traced to the one that the Bible calls our enemy and adversary.

The Devil couldn't care less about how you are hurting or how he hurts your children as he tears your family apart. He will not keep his hands off your home. His goal is to mislead you and stage your home for doom and destruction.

Just as much as God loves unity and teamwork in families, Satan hates it. Satan likes to see marriages struggle, suffer, and fail. He does this through the deception of myths—lies, wrong thinking, false assumptions. He is a master at using myths to convince you that something is right when it's really wrong and that your spouse is the enemy.

When I finally understood this—that Satan has no positive concern about my family and that he is out to destroy my marriage—it transformed the way I treated Rhonda. I finally understood that I was fighting spiritual battles every day over the holy ground of marriage.

RIGHT THINKING, RIGHT ACTIONS

Since you're reading this book, it's probably safe for me to make a few assumptions about you. Either you are about to be married, you're newly married, or are a marriage veteran. Perhaps you feel anxious about the direction your marriage is headed. Maybe you're considering walking out because you feel that your marriage is no longer fulfilling—or even that it's the marriage from hell.

In all of this, perhaps you've lost hope.

The good news is that you can hope again. A bad marriage is not like a piece of fruit that goes bad and has to be tossed in the garbage. It's more like a person with a serious illness who gets some timely help . . . and begins to heal and regain strength. Sick marriages can heal. I've seen it happen time after time.

I've seen old lies jerked from the soil like long-rooted weeds. I've seen truth take root and begin to flower. I've seen love return like April sunshine after a long winter. You can call it a reconciliation or a restoration or a rebuilt home.

I always call it a miracle.

My sincere prayer is that this book will cause you to take a closer look at the myths you believe—sometimes without even knowing that you believe them. Your marriage is too valuable to be driven by wrong thinking. You need the truth that will lead you to right feelings and right actions. Jesus said only the truth gives us true freedom (John 8:32). The truth will lead you to serve one another and nurture your mate's spiritual well-being. Truth will also cause you to fulfill your lifetime commitment to God and to your mate, no matter how hard it gets.

Even seasoned couples who make marriage look effortless admit that they've had their fair share of distorted thoughts and feelings. When my wife reflects on our early days together, she reminds me, "Mitch, you were the most naïve man I ever met. You were really messed up, but I married you because I knew you had a good heart."

I think her marriage to me was a kind of spiritual benevolence—a way to save me from myself. No matter what kind of benevolence I feel it was, I'm glad she became my wife. Gratefully, God has molded our relationship into one of the strongest I know.

In spite of Satan's best attempts to destroy your marriage, my desire is to help you make it as great as God intended. I want to guide you through a minefield of myths with God's Word as our source of truth. I want to help you turn your marriage around. Let's get started.

Chapter Two

"Attitudes Don't Really Count"

"Remember that whatever you do in life,

ninety percent of it is half mental."

Yogi Berra[1]

IN NOVEMBER OF THE TENTH YEAR of our marriage, Rhonda and I were discussing a sensitive issue that comes up every year: where we were going to spend Christmas.

By this time in our marriage, we knew which topics created sparks, and this was one of them. As a result, we were both armed for battle.

Rhonda responded to a statement I'd made by saying, "Now you've got an attitude. Stop talking to me like I'm a child! You're being very condescending."

Without really thinking, I snapped back, "Hey! This has nothing to do with my attitude! Don't play that card! We went to your folks' for Thanksgiving, so we're going to mine for Christmas!"

We didn't know that our then five-year-old daughter, Hannah, was in the living room watching TV and listening to our conversation. Suddenly, her tiny voice rang out, "Whoa! Whoa! Hold it right there, Dad! Barney just said that attitude is the most important thing in life."

Hannah had a point. So did Barney.

Attitudes and the thoughts that form them are important, especially in marriage. You can attend every marriage conference available and read every book on romantic love out there, but if your marriage is based on destructive attitudes, it's likely that nothing will help.

CHANGE YOUR MIND, CHANGE YOUR MARRIAGE

Thoughts and attitudes are like the engine of a train and our emotions and behavior are like the caboose.

Thoughts help form and determine your attitudes toward marriage. They determine how you feel about your mate as well as how you feel about being married in general. Thoughts can inspire hope—or take it away. Changing the way you think is like a locomotive that switches tracks and heads in a new direction, taking the rest of the train—behavior, actions, and habits—right along with it.

Paul obviously didn't have a train in mind when he offered his heartfelt instructions to the Christians in Rome—but it's still a useful metaphor. Pleading with the Romans to change their thoughts and actions, he said, "I urge you, brothers, in view of God's mercy, to offer your bodies as living sacrifices, holy and pleasing to God. . . . Do not conform any longer to the pattern of this world, but be transformed by the renewing of your mind. . . . Do not think of yourself more highly than you ought, but rather think of yourself with sober judgment" (Romans 12:1–3).

The apostle is speaking about a major mind shift here. The word *transform* comes from the same basic root for the English word *metamorphosis*. As larvae go through a radical change to become butterflies, so must we sometimes radically change our minds in order to have a healthy faith and marriage.

When we do make this change, we will not think of ourselves higher than we should (v. 3), and our judgments (perceptions, beliefs, conclusions, attitudes) will be sober, clear, and accurate. *Transforming our thinking can lead us to the right behaviors* (vv. 9–21). The right behavior will then lead to the outcomes we want such as peace, intimacy, and oneness. The more we understand this principle, the more positive impact it will have on our relationships.

One of my good friends, Dr. Gary Rosberg, is one of the most spiritual men I know. When I grow up I want to be just like him. Whenever we're together, talk on the phone, correspond by e-mail, or chat after I finish a radio interview on his show, the last thing he always says to me is, "Hey Mitch, guard your heart, brother." This is another way of saying, "Be very careful to protect your mind from the wrong stuff. Put the right things in your mind. Protect it. Shield it from the bad influences." Just recently, after the birth of my first grandchild, Gary's message to me was: "Mitch, guard your heart, brother. The stakes just got higher."

I know Gary means for me to guard my heart in every area of life, including my relationship with Rhonda. Like a computer, if I put the right things into my mind, the right things will likely come out. Gary understands this. He knows that if my thinking is on track, then the rest of my life will be too.

Our Creator commands spouses—particularly husbands—to guard their hearts and thinking so that they do not forsake the wife of their youth (Malachi 2:14–16). God is serious about how we think and behave in our marriage. We should be too.

Sure, our actions may be due to "unthinking" habits we've fallen into. You may leave the bathroom messy every day without even thinking about it. Just part of the routine, right?

But if you really reflect on that habit, you may discover that there was a particular thought, belief, value, or idea that led you to the action—or at minimum maintained it. Maybe you thought at some time previously, *I did this before I was married, so I should be able to keep on doing it.* Or, *What's the big deal? I'll clean up later, but now I'm in a hurry.*

Sometimes, though, our distorted thinking can lead to consequences much more severe than squabbles about bathrooms.

THE DANGER OF DISTORTED THINKING

If you are angry, afraid, resentful, jealous, or depressed—in other words, if you are struggling with negative emotions—the fault may lie in your thinking. Cognitive therapists operate on the theory that distorted thinking lies at the root of most of these negative emotions. These therapists help their clients identify the distorted thinking, understand what is distorted about it, and then correct it so that emotional healing can begin.

Here are some common distorted thoughts. Do any of them sound familiar?

- *I must be approved and loved by all people.*
- *If things don't go the way I expect them to, then it's catastrophic.*
- *It's easier to avoid a problem than to deal with conflict.*
- *What has happened in the past will determine the future.*
- *If I make a mistake, it means that I am incompetent and that I am inferior to others.*
- *Things always turn out this way.*
- *You always act this way.*
- *You never treat me the way I deserve to be treated.*
- *You should always feel or act a certain way.*

Research shows that these thoughts can lead to serious problems, among them addictions and depression.[2] I know.

I've struggled with depression for most of my life, so I'm very familiar with distorted thinking. While growing up, I suspected I had a problem, but counseling was not smiled upon then, and I had no idea how to get help.

I bet you can guess what happened when I got married. You got it. I didn't check my depression at the door. My moodiness, anger, and negativity moved into the Temple home.

After ten years of marriage, Rhonda and I were desperate.

I was extremely depressed and I worried about everything—even in my sleep. I often woke up in the middle of the night in a cold sweat, but I couldn't go back to sleep because the anxiety from my dreams kept me awake. Sleep deprivation caused me to be contentious and on edge. I lost forty pounds, became physically ill, and experienced constant nausea. When I thought I had cancer or another terminal illness, I visited numerous doctors without a diagnosis. Finally, an internal medicine specialist from India gave me an answer.

"Mr. Temple," he said in accented English, "you don't have a physical problem. You have an emotional problem. You have developed an anxiety disorder, and you are also very depressed. You must get help or you may die."

After weeks of denial, I knew he was right, so I finally got the help I needed.

The counselor I visited convinced me to take depression medication, even though I was terrified of becoming addicted. I spoke with my good friend Jeff Mathis, MD, who alleviated my concerns. He said that most antidepressants are not addictive and should be a bridge, not a crutch, to help navigate through a dark emotional valley.

Because my marriage, family, faith, and job were on the line, I was willing to do whatever was necessary. The result? Over time, I became a better husband. And the way I saw myself, Rhonda, and others improved.

I was transformed.

Through my experience I learned that because I suffered from depression, I could not see myself or my wife realistically. I felt as if I were stumbling around in dark rooms—wearing sunglasses. I couldn't see myself as God sees me. I felt that I could not be good enough, faithful enough, or spiritual enough—no matter what the Bible says.

These kinds of beliefs, based on myths and distorted thinking, led me to depression and hopelessness. They can also lead us to accept Satan's lie that you are not worthy of grace and can cause us to act in ways that we'll regret.

This is typical in a marriage where a spouse is depressed. Though a depressed husband is committed to marriage, he won't feel good about his wife and, therefore, won't treat her well. If the nondepressed wife does not understand what is happening, she will make the situation worse by assuming that her husband is mean or doesn't care about the marriage or that he can easily change how he feels and acts.

In reality, change can be almost impossible for a depressed person. Until the depressed spouse receives proper treatment, he or she cannot interact with you in a healthy way.

Depression is a very serious illness, which if left untreated can destroy a marriage in a short period of time. Many marriages today are in trouble because one or both spouses struggle with severe depression. Until these couples address and treat depression, it will be difficult to learn new relational skills to strengthen their marriage.

If you suspect that you, or your spouse, suffer from depression, seek help together. Focus on the Family provides free counseling referrals.[3]

(A caveat is in order here. Depression and other emotional problems *can* be caused by factors other than distorted thinking. Chemical and sugar imbalances, stress, lack of sleep, even thyroid disorders can also be precipitators of depression. When issues like these are involved, they must be assessed, diagnosed, and treated by a medical professional.)

You may not struggle with depression. But distorted thinking, because it is so subtle and rooted in the way you look at yourself and your spouse, has the potential to eat away at your marriage.

THE RUTS IN YOUR MIND

Distorted thinking (we should never have conflict; my spouse should meet all my needs) can lay "ruts" in your mind.

As pioneers headed West in their wagons, they tended to follow the same trails as those who had gone before them. Eventually, the soil became compressed and ruts appeared. These ruts wore so deep that they still exist today.[4] In northeastern Oregon, you can actually walk out behind a museum and see the literal Oregon Trail.

Add a little mud to such deep ruts, and you can well imagine a covered wagon getting its wheels stuck, so immobilized that even a team of oxen or horses couldn't pull it out. We can guess it took a little shovel work—and a lot of manhandling—to get back on the trail again.

Or if you've ever gotten stuck in deep snow, spinning your wheels, needing a push or some traction—you know how difficult it can be to pull out.

Marriage ruts can be the same. When you and your spouse disagree

. . . or get hurt . . . or become frustrated . . . or reach an impasse . . . *the easiest thing to do is what you have always done*! Human nature tends to follow the same patterns of interactions and reactions over and over again—especially when we're under stress.

Like the early pioneers, we might know we're stuck, but not know what to do about it. Eventually, distorted thinking, attitudes, and behavior become a normal part of the journey together.

And we ride the ruts into the sunset.

Sometimes I realize I'm doing the same hurtful, nonproductive things over and over, and it isn't helping a thing! I can hear myself make the same useless comments I made last time—and get no more traction with them than I did then!

You want an example? Easy.

For many years in our marriage every time my dear wife disagreed with me, I got defensive. Instead of trying to understand her point of view, I *reacted*. Maybe blew up.

That, my friend, is a rut. And it got deeper every time I spun my wheels in it.

Rhonda gets into ruts as well. She manages our finances and does a wonderful job. But sometimes when money is tight, she tries to shield me by fixing the problem on her own. When I probe to find out what's wrong, she doesn't want to talk about it. I pressure her and she becomes more frustrated. I get defensive, she gets defensive, and then we argue, criticize, and withdraw. We have learned new ways to handle things, but we resort back to the past.

Same lousy ruts, same nonresults.

Mike and Ellen

OUR FRIENDS MIKE AND ELLEN are also familiar with marriage ruts. One night over coffee, Ellen mentioned an ongoing pattern that was wreaking havoc in their marriage.

Ellen stays home with the kids, and by the time Mike arrives in the evening, she is exhausted. She wants him to jump into the parenting ring and do a little fighting. Because Mike works only one mile away, he has had little time to unwind. As a result, he's on edge when he walks through the door. When Ellen unloads on Mike everything the kids have done wrong during the day, he feels even more aggravated. As Ellen vents her frustrations, Mike sees her lips moving, but he doesn't hear a word. All he hears is nagging. Ellen picks up on Mike's frustration and assumes that he doesn't care. The ruts in their marriage road have been established. Ellen gets angry and doesn't talk to Mike, and Mike withdraws into his study and spends the evening on the computer. Sadly, the kids play alone.

After hearing their story, Rhonda and I could relate. We fell into a similar rut earlier in our marriage. We finally recognized the unhealthy pattern we had gotten into and implemented some changes that worked for us. We offered what worked for us to Mike and Ellen. We suggested that Ellen give Mike at least fifteen minutes after he arrives home for time to unwind. We also encouraged Ellen to break her complaints into smaller chunks. Most people cannot handle a truckload of bad news all at once.

Ellen agreed. Mike also agreed to give Ellen some time to unwind after his arrival by taking the kids to the park.

We also helped Mike and Ellen take a look at their negative attitudes, such as: "He doesn't understand"; "He doesn't care what I go through"; "She always acts this way"; and "She doesn't respect me anymore."

Over the next weeks, Ellen and Mike joined forces to move out of the old ruts they'd created, and they developed new, healthier ways of relating.

"MY MARRIAGE IS KILLING ME!"

Tara, a young lady at the church I was working for at the time, approached me one day after church and asked to speak with me. "You've got to help me. I know in my heart that my attitude is wrong, but—I can't help it. It's how I feel. My marriage is *killing* me. It's so bad. I just want to give up. I'm tired of fighting. I'm tired of being the only one trying."

Tara wiped tears from her cheeks. I knew Tara likes to be direct and she is a good friend, so I decided to shoot straight with her.

"Tara, can I be real with you?" I asked.

"Yes, please. I'm at the end of my rope. Just tell me anything that will help me," she pleaded.

"Do you really want to make your marriage better?"

"Well, if it can be. I know it's what's best for the kids and I know it's what's right. I know God hates divorce."

"Tara, then here's the key. You have to begin with your attitude. You have to stop thinking that your marriage is over and that it can't be changed. If you keep thinking and saying that it's over, your feelings and actions will follow and your marriage will eventually fail."

Tara's tears flowed unabated.

"Do me a favor," I said. "For one day, stop focusing on your marriage ending and focus on saving your marriage—even if you don't believe it's possible. Can you stop thinking about it being over for at least twenty-four hours? Will you at least consider that your marriage might just work?"

Tara looked surprised; it wasn't what she expected from me. I'm usually more passive and empathetic in my approach.

She sighed. "Well, all I can do is try. I don't know what else to do."

Not only did she try, but she made great strides in turning her heart around. The next day, she called my office. "Well, no miracle has happened yet," she said, "but I do feel better. I did what you told me to do. For a few hours, I stopped obsessing about my marriage ending and started to think about changing my attitude versus trying to change Matt's. I stopped praying that God would end the pain and get me out of it and started praying that God would change my heart and restore my joy. It really made a difference in how I looked at Matt and the future of our marriage."

I was thrilled. "Good, that's the first step," I said. "Now, let me help you with the next."

In a series of meetings, I convinced Tara that if she continued to work on her attitude, then her actions regarding her marriage would open up new possibilities for changes in Matt. Like most people, Tara felt that 99 percent of her marital problems were her spouse's fault. Over time, she had convinced herself that Matt was the reason her marriage was headed south and that her actions and attitudes had nothing to do with it. Though she hadn't seen any valid signs of adultery, Tara even imagined that Matt was cheating. Her thoughts spiraled downward, producing more and more destructive thinking and behavior.

And the more she allowed her thoughts to spin in that rut, the deeper it became.

As Tara made changes in attitude toward Matt, he noticed. He appreciated her increased respect and grace when he made mistakes. She stopped reacting in the same ways as before. Within a few short weeks, Matt came to counseling with Tara. We worked on basic attitude changes, actions, and how they could interact without arguing. Changes slowly occurred in their hearts and even their everyday interactions improved. They're happier than ever now, and it all started with changes in thinking and attitude.

Perhaps you're thinking, *This doesn't apply to me. My attitude is stellar. I'm right on track.* Fair enough. But do yourself a favor and take this quick checkup. How many of these statements have you recently thought or said to your spouse? Put a check by those that apply.

- ☐ "If you disagree with something I said or did, it means you don't love me."
- ☐ "If you disappoint me, I'll make your life miserable."
- ☐ "It's no use to keep trying to talk through our problems. We always end up fighting."
- ☐ "You'll never forgive me for what I did."
- ☐ "Because you make the same mistakes over and over, it means you don't care."

- ☐ "It's always going to be this way. Nothing will ever change."

☐ "Our marriage has never been good. You've never really loved me."

☐ "You shouldn't feel that way."

☐ "You always treat me the same way."

☐ "You never show me you love me."

☐ "It's always about you."

☐ "You are never wrong."

☐ "I'm never right."

☐ "It's your fault I feel this way. You make me act this way."

☐ "Because our marriage doesn't look like _____'s marriage, it's not right."

☐ "I'm not being treated like I should be."

☐ "I'm not happy . . . so I have the right to treat you the way I do."

☐ "You're not meeting my needs; I have a right to find someone else who will."

☐ "I'm not in love with you anymore—so the commitment means nothing to me."

☐ "This marriage is keeping me from living up to my potential."

☐ "If you would just change, our marriage would be okay."

☐ "The kids would be better off without their mom and dad fighting all the time."

Do any words in this list sound vaguely familiar? Could it be that your attitude—or your marriage—has begun a slow drift in an unhelpful, unhappy direction? Now is the best time I can think of to get back on course.

ADRIFT ON THE BAY

One day when I was fishing in Florida, it was getting late in the evening. I was tired and decided to take a rest. I closed my eyes, laid down my pole, propped my feet up, and drifted off to sleep. A short time later, I was startled awake by the sound of heavy traffic.

Oh no, I'm in the middle of a highway and I'm about to be killed! Then, I remembered I was in the boat. Because I didn't put out the anchor, I had drifted more than two miles in the bay underneath Interstate 10, where cars were rushing overhead.

When you lose hope in your marriage, you drift as I did on the bay. Emotions, circumstances, and myths are the winds that move you, not truth, which is the foundation of hope. Hopeless faith and hopeless marriages are always vulnerable to ruin.

One dictionary defines hope as "the happy anticipation of good." [5]

Hope motivates us to make positive choices in life and marriage and to be in right relationship with Christ and His people. God's Word says, "We have this hope as an anchor for the soul, firm and secure" (Hebrews 6:19). When you lose hope, your soul is like a boat lost at sea without an anchor.

Jesus, who sees into the depths of the human heart, knows what it takes to restore hope in a person's life.

Remember the story of how He met the Samaritan woman at the well in John chapter 4? Jesus knew who she was, that she'd had multiple husbands, and that she believed religious myths. He knew that her attitude about the past was seemingly hopeless. I wonder if the tape she played in her mind went something like this: "There's no hope for me. I've made too many mistakes and I don't deserve to be helped."

But after this woman spent time with Jesus, hope filled her thoughts. Though He instructed her to change the way she lived in the past, He loved her as a sinner and accepted her as a person.

And she came right up out of her deep ruts of bad thoughts and emotions.

She even ran to tell others about her interaction with Jesus—"Come see a man who told me everything I ever did. Could this be the

Christ?" (v. 29).

Spending time with Jesus can have a huge effect on our thinking, attitudes, and behavior.

Don't allow anyone, including the Devil, to convince you that the health and security of your marriage has nothing to do with your thinking, attitude, and beliefs! Truth that is based on the teachings of Jesus and the Bible is truth that can completely transform your heart, life, and relationships.

Chapter Three

"I Need to Change My Spouse"

*"I finally figured it out. I know why we struggled
early in our marriage—I married a dog!"*

Bertha

MARRIED FOR OVER THIRTY YEARS, Bertha and Dan attended a class I taught on personality differences. As part of the teaching, I used an assessment tool developed by my friend Dr. John Trent, based on four animals. The four personality types—lions, otters, golden retrievers, and beavers—help couples understand personality styles and preferences.

With characteristic wit, John explains how people who score high on the *L*, or *Lion* scale, are typically assertive. You'll find these folks in management or director positions because they enjoy running, directing, and starring in the show. Unfortunately, they are often impatient with those who are meticulous, and they tend to be the "horn honkers" in traffic. These are the folks who test the religion of mild-mannered people.

People who score high on the *O* or *Otter* scale are the "get the party cranked up" types. You'll find them potluck hopping and talking to as many different people as possible at social events because they thrive on personal interaction. And if others won't talk, they'll ask questions to strangers or talk to themselves!

I recently saw an *Otter* in a clothing store. Because she was alone and had no one to talk to, she chatted with herself as she sashayed in front of the mirror. She asked, "Does this cute blouse look good on you?"

"Oh baby, you are one hot chick, buy it!"

I couldn't help but laugh.

Otters resist routine because they thrive on change. They're also inspirational and creative, but tend to procrastinate. They won't pack their suitcase until the last minute. They wait until the night before the exam to crack open a textbook. They embrace the philosophy "Don't worry. Be happy!" and may wonder why others are so unnerved by deadlines.

My wife, Rhonda, is a typical *Otter*. For years I let her spontaneity drive me crazy because I am a control freak about schedules. She will wait until the last minute to do things, yet somehow she always gets them done. Twenty-six years later I admire this about her because she's taught me to lighten up and live on the edge now and then.

If you have a spouse who falls into the *G* or *Golden Retriever* category, you might say, "She's so sweet," or "He's the kindest man in the world." Your spouse is most likely a good listener and sympathetic, which is why people call him or her when they're in trouble or need a listening ear.

Golden Retrievers may hate taking something back to the retail store because they don't want to cause trouble. It's often hard for them to say no to church committees, and they usually bring the snacks to soccer practice each week because they don't want to ask someone else to do it. Because they're compassionate, they can start out with twenty dollars in change in the morning but by evening they've given to all the beggars in town. They are hardworking, loyal employees and tend to stay at one job for a long time.

I put the *G* in *Golden Retriever*. Unfortunately, I am often more concerned about what other people think of me than I am of the Lord's opinion of me. It's pitiful. I'm learning to domesticate this part of my personality as I grow up, but it is hard. On the positive side, most people like me so they pat me on the head—just like a dog.

Beavers are generally structured and dependable. They show up first at events so they can sit toward the front. They actually make their beds and often win the prize for the "yard of the month." They may label their Tupperware and tape the lids to the corresponding containers.

These are also the men who put their workshop screws in tiny jars and label them according to length and purpose. They take orders well and follow instructions to the T. They read maps. Because they are structured, they complete projects before they tackle new ones.

I encourage couples to read John's book or visit the Ministry Insights website.[1] The Marriage Insight tool is a fun way to understand your mate's personality.

As I said earlier, "The more you understand your mate's personality, the more you can accept him or her, and the more you accept, the more you heal and thrive." Realizing this helped move me from resenting Rhonda's personality to embracing, appreciating, and even admiring it.

Though Bertha, quoted above, was joking about her husband, Dan, she nailed his personality type. He is a dog—a *Golden Retriever*. He is compassionate, quiet, mild-mannered, and affectionate. Bertha on the other hand is . . . can you guess? Yep, an *Otter*! She thrives on a good time and is consistently the life of the party.

During our class, I never knew what Bertha was going to say. If Dan got a chance to talk when Bertha took a breath between sentences, what he said was pretty profound. Everybody listened when he spoke. They are like "Ying and Yang"—opposite in personality, but they have a great marriage.

Bertha said she was attracted to Dan because she came from a family of four sisters and three brothers. Everyone in her house talked at once. She found Dan refreshing because she didn't have to compete with him for talk time. If anything, she had to poke him on occasions to see if he was still alive.

Dan and Bertha

AS I MENTIONED, DAN AND BERTHA are two of the most mismatched people in the world; they are like night and day. But when someone asks them if they love and like each other, they always squeeze each other tight and say, "You betcha." They are 100 percent committed to their marriage—and it shows.

Are Dan and Bertha perfect? No.

Do their personality differences sometimes cause problems? Sure.

Their differences caused severe problems, especially in the early years of their marriage when they bought into myths many of us fall for, such as: "I can change my spouse."

Though Bertha loved her husband's serene demeanor, after living with Dan for two or three months, she became enormously bored. She did everything she could to light a fire under Dan, including starting arguments just to make him angry. "I may have gotten more than I bargained for, but when I made Dan mad, at least I knew he was still alive," she said.

Dan said that trying to change Bertha was like "trying to put high heels on an elephant"—almost impossible. "The more I tried to change her, the more she resisted. The more I tried to temper her ways, the more she dug her heels in. The more she resisted, the more I resented and disliked her."

Dan reached a point where he became embarrassed to take Bertha out. "I resorted to lying to make excuses as to why I couldn't go to social events with her." When Bertha figured out that Dan was being dishonest, she began mistrusting him in other areas of their marriage. She racked her brain to make sense of what was behind Dan's out-of-character behavior, and she became cynical about how he wasn't acting like the man she married.

Instead of buying into the myth that they could change each other, here's how they worked out their differences. After many "silent nights, unholy nights," Bertha said they both felt they needed God's wisdom to bring them back together. Out of desperation, they started praying together. Things started to change for the better when their prayers led them to spend time walking through their neighborhood in the evening, long drives in the car, and sitting at the table after dinner to discuss their differences in an effort to understand each other.

They learned to manage problems and head off misunderstandings at the pass. For example, Bertha said if they felt a certain topic of discussion might be a little volatile, they went out for coffee so they wouldn't be tempted to yell at each other like crazy people.

The more they prayed and talked, the more wisdom and understanding God gave them regarding their diversity. The more they understood each other's unique ways, the more they accepted and appreciated one other. They became students of personalities and read everything they could find about personality types.

Dan realized that one of Bertha's core personality traits is her love for people and conversation. So he knew that if he forced her to avoid social events, it would kill her spirit. That's the last thing he really wanted to do. Instead, he embraced his wife's need for social interaction, even when he didn't necessarily feel like it.

Dan developed a few coping mechanisms to handle Bertha's social personality. They still make him chuckle. "Sometimes I went to events with Bertha and after twenty minutes or so I would sneak out to the car to catch a nap. I always set my watch so, I could slip back in after about half an hour. Bertha never noticed. When I would come back in, she was still on the same subject!"

Bertha accepted Dan's need to escape and that he could only handle crowds for short periods of time. She knew that although crowds energized her, they drained Dan. So Bertha honored Dan's inclination not to be a party animal. Before arriving at social events, Bertha learned to set her watch as a reminder of when it was time to go. She knew she had a tendency to get caught up in conversations and wouldn't know when to shut up and leave. Occasionally Dan waved his watch in the air to alert Bertha that he was at his social limit. Other times, Bertha knew Dan was ready to go but she would hold up five fingers to request five more minutes of social pleasure.

Great compromise technique, huh?

To their credit, Dan and Bertha reinvented their relationship so they wouldn't get the same negative results as before.

Instead of buying into this myth of changing the other, this couple learned "to dance." They viewed these simple adjustments as little "inconveniences" that they could easily give up in order to gain the greater outcome—peace, intimacy, and oneness. Bertha said that they learned the value of "giving up in order to get." They learned to sacrifice little battles in order to win the war. What a great philosophy for couples to live by.

When you can learn the principles Dan and Bertha learned, you not only begin to dance, you start to waltz. You connect with your spouse in ways that you may have thought were impossible.

It is all about learning when to move in one direction and when to move in the other, when to follow and when to take the lead. Making changes in marriage not only depends on understanding and accepting personality, but also in letting go of pride. Pride will hinder marriage progress in almost any scenario. This is especially true when working out differences or deciding whether to compromise or stand your ground.

Pride causes a spouse to say, "I'm not the problem. You are the problem. My personality is perfect. Yours is screwed up." Pride pushes selfish points of views such as "Your irritations are more irritating than mine." A proud spouse also says, "I will not change in areas where I know I really can, but you definitely need to change."

The Scriptures are pretty self-explanatory: "The Lord detests all the proud of heart" (Proverbs 16:5). I am sure that one of the reasons God hates pride is because pride separates us not only from our Creator, but it wipes out the "one-flesh" piece of marriage. Pride is a strong culprit of ongoing division and deep, deep disconnection between couples.

Prideful husbands stick to their guns when they should lay them down and be humble. Prideful wives stand their ground when they need to sit down and shut up. But husbands and wives bathed in humility and wisdom know when to speak and when not to speak. They see themselves as imperfect, sinful people. They embrace grace and therefore give it freely.

How many Christian couples have you seen that seemed to have it all together—and then all of the sudden they fall apart? I would suspect that pride had something to do with it, don't you? Again, the Bible sums it up so well: "Pride goes before destruction, a haughty spirit before a fall" (Proverbs 16:18).

Understand that you will fail when learning to dance. Don't freak out when you "step on each other's toes." Learn to say, "I'm sorry, I made a mistake," and move on. If anything, compete for who says I am sorry first. Commit to work through and embrace your differences as challenges to conquer instead of getting frustrated and giving up.

When your focus is on changing the other, you can expect turmoil, disappointment, and hurt. Think about how you react when a boss tries to change you by forcing you to do something that you are not capable of doing. It causes you anger and frustration. You begin to dislike your boss. The same is true when you try to change your spouse. But when you start to "get it" and begin to accept one another and are open to change in areas where you can, intimacy skyrockets.

RELATIONAL NEARSIGHTEDNESS (RN)

For most of my life I was extremely nearsighted. I really can't remember not wearing glasses as a kid. In the eighth grade my ophthalmologist made me stop playing any kind of contact sports because nearsightedness had stretched my retinas to the point of almost breaking. Even *with* glasses I didn't have very good vision. If I took my glasses off, I was dangerous not only to myself but also to those around me. I couldn't see anything clearly over four to five inches from my face. Forget minutiae and details, I was almost blind. If I couldn't get extremely close to something, I missed textures, colors, and details. I spent most of my life tripping, stumbling, busting my shins, and missing beauty. Plus people made fun of me most of my life for wearing glasses with ugly, thick lenses. By the time I was an adult, my nearsightedness had "progressed" to the point where I was considered legally blind.

That was my thorn in the flesh. I had to live with it. There was no other alternative such as surgery at the time.

When Rhonda married me, she knew I was extremely nearsighted. Fortunately, by the time we met I wore special contacts, so "my stellar looks" could emerge from behind the thick glasses.

What Rhonda didn't know was that I also suffered from *relational* nearsightedness. Everything had to be my way. I had to be right. I could only see what benefited me. My philosophy was that my personality was okay—but Rhonda's needed a tremendous amount of work.

Physical nearsightedness and relational nearsightedness (RN) have a lot in common. When people develop RN, they can't see far beyond themselves. They tend to miss the reality that the world is larger than just what involves them. Instead of seeing others' needs as equally or more important than theirs, it's all about them. These are the spouses who completely miss how their attitudes, behavior, and decisions affect the other. They also miss the beauty and variety of those around them. They are oblivious to their own faults. And they tend to be harsh and rigid with their mates and often with their children.

Pride and relational nearsightedness fit together like a glove on a hand. Pride feeds nearsightedness. Nearsightedness feeds selfish behavior. Selfish behavior creates distance between godly couples and hinders progress.

Maybe that's why the words of the apostle Peter caught my attention so forcefully not long ago. Writing to a group of suffering believers scattered across the Roman Empire, the old fisherman had an interesting observation. He said that if we fail to apply the Christian graces to our daily lives—faith, goodness, knowledge, self-control, perseverance, godliness, kindness, and love—then we become blind and nearsighted and can't see far past ourselves (2 Peter 1:5–9).

The Greek word Peter used for *nearsighted* in this passage is the same root word from which we get our English word *myopia*—yet another word for nearsightedness.

What Peter seems to be saying here is that when Christians don't fill their lives with the right kind of thinking and actions, they get self-focused, self-centered. They see the obvious, physical things—things that benefit themselves, but they miss the eternal, the sacred. They focus on the immediate, the here and now, only seeing as far as the world around them. Their shortsightedness leaves them blind to the bigger picture, the need to become more like Christ.

Sound familiar? Most of us struggle with myopia in our faith. Many of us also struggle with nearsightedness in our marriage. I certainly have.

Rhonda loves people and enjoys talking about her life. Occasionally, she also enjoys talking about semipersonal things—and that was the rub for me early in our marriage.

I am a preacher's kid and was taught to keep my mouth shut about anything that had to do with family matters. "If people know our business," my dad always said, "they will use it against us." Unfortunately, he was right most of the time. Church members did in fact use family information to hurt us from time to time.

Though I believe there is a need to protect some private matters, I was at one extreme and Rhonda was at the other. She trusted everybody, and I trusted no one. She expected others to be trustworthy; I prided myself in a healthy (and safe) skepticism.

My anger with Rhonda often flared when we were around church people. Because Rhonda was the church social butterfly and talked to everyone, she eventually shared something I felt was private. I now recognize that it was never anything too personal; I just had a nearsighted view of what it meant to keep confidentiality.

On the ride home from church one day, Rhonda could sense my anger, and because she didn't want to hear my criticisms, she became quiet. I responded in kind to punish her with silence. In the South we call it pouting. Although we may have thought we were avoiding confrontation by our silence, it was only making us angrier.

I knew Rhonda recognized that I was upset, but I thought, *She doesn't care enough to talk about it or apologize.* So, I decided the best thing to do was to change her. *After all,* I reasoned, *we have to protect our career and ministry.* I was certain my view was right and was the one we were going live by.

Boy, was I wrong.

In my efforts to reform the "flawed Rhonda," I hurt her to the core. Every time I look back, I feel great shame about my behavior. I said and did things that broke her heart and spirit. The message I gave her was that I didn't love her as she was created. Refusing to see and note her many positive traits, I became obsessed with what I regarded as her negative ones.

I wanted Rhonda to change into someone she could not become. I bought into the myth that I could change her.

My physical myopia through the years of my life had been painfully obvious. The coke-bottle glasses gave that away. My relational nearsightedness was not as obvious, at least to others. And yet it almost robbed our marriage of its beauty and goodness. It almost caused the woman I loved with all my heart to stop loving me.

After months of living like this, we talked less, trusted less, and were intimate less often. Sex became very rare. To compensate for our struggling relationship, Rhonda invested in outside friendships at church; I invested in work and extended family. I could help other people at church with their problems, but I was so blind that I refused to see my own and deal with them as a Christian leader should.

In my late thirties, a group of church friends, to show their appreciation for my service to the church and community, collected money to pay for laser surgery that would correct my vision. I will always be grateful for that gesture.

At that time, laser surgery was pretty risky on patients with extreme myopia. In fact, my surgeon had never operated on someone with such an extreme case of nearsightedness. There was a possibility that the surgery wouldn't help, and even that it could cause me to lose my eyesight completely. But I was willing to take the risk.

About four days after the surgery, when the incisions were just about healed, I went outside just before dusk. I immediately noticed how brilliant and clear everything was. I was like a kid at Disney World the first time. I could see the leaves on the trees! I looked up at the moon. It was no longer a fuzzy glow, but it had texture, and beautiful shades of gray and white! I was thrilled.

I saw beauty in things I had never noticed before. When I looked out my office window, I could see shades of brown and swirling lines on the fence posts. I was surprised that the grass had individual blades with rich shades of green and pale yellow. When I opened my hands, I saw curves and lines in my palms. When I walked around staring at my palms, people thought I was nuts, but it was a whole new world for me.

I experienced clear vision for the first time since childhood.

A few months after the surgery, I raked my sweet wife over the coals for something that irritated me. She listened for a few minutes, then looked me squarely in the eyes, with tears in hers, and said, "Mitch, you are still blind when it comes to our marriage. I wish someone could help you with your other blindness."

Ouch. I was stung to the core. I experienced anger, then hurt, and then anger again. I was offended, so as usual, I withdrew, with Rhonda's words ringing in my ears.

Eventually I had no choice; I had to look beyond myself.

I realized Rhonda was right. I had a bad case of RN. I had focused for so long on changing her that I missed the beautiful way the good Lord made her. If I wanted to change my marriage, I had to change my thinking and behavior—I had to change my heart.

Thankfully, I did change, but it didn't happen overnight.

I read everything I could get my hands on about understanding your mate's personality, accepting his or her differences, communication, and even how to express appreciation within marriage.

I scrutinized every emotion. I questioned my thoughts and how I reacted to her comments. I learned about sending subtle messages through body language.

I asked myself questions such as, "Should I be feeling this way? Have I overreacted? Are my feelings accurate? Do I need to look at other facts or possibilities?"

At the end of each day, I reviewed the things I had said to Rhonda and how I had behaved toward her. If I felt convicted that I had hurt her, I apologized. I was determined to change myself, no longer her.

Instead of being so focused on my needs, I started focusing on the broader, bigger, clearer view of my marriage. My rights, perspective, and ideas moved to the background as I made changes that allowed me to see the true image of my wife. I began to see her the way her Creator sees her: "beautiful" in every way (Ecclesiastes 3:11).

What about you? Do you see your spouse with clear vision, the way God sees him or her? Or do you see your spouse through distorted beliefs?

WHAT YOU CAN'T CHANGE

As we've noted in the last few pages, there are some things about your spouse that will never change—and probably shouldn't! When it comes to core personality issues, you can't force a turtle to sprint like a rabbit. God didn't make turtles to sprint; they were made to process life in a slower, more leisurely way. Or to put it in Dr. Trent's terms, you can't make a lion out of a golden retriever. He might rise to the occasion and growl at someone who threatens his family, but day in and day out, he's going to be lovable and friendly.

Unchangeable differences are ones that couples must learn to *understand* and *manage*, not change. Let's look at few others areas you can't change.

• *Gender.* Here's something profound: men are different from women.

You've heard this before. But let me assure you, thousands of couples divorce each year because they forget this fact. They expect their mate to think, feel, and act like they do in every situation. Some divorce because they don't understand those differences—and can never get past them, let alone appreciate them.

I once worked with a young husband who was ready to walk out on his wife because he couldn't understand her monthly mood changes. Unfortunately, he took her monthly cycle personally and thought she was about to "go postal." He actually believed that he had made a mistake and married a psychopathic woman because of this misunderstanding.

Because of negative family experiences while growing up, he said he wasn't going to live with a crazy woman no matter what he promised God or his preacher. Raised with two brothers, he'd never encountered PMS before, and his parents never talked of such things. (He must have also slept through health class in school.)

I spent time explaining what she was experiencing—physiologically and emotionally. This was all new information to this young husband. His reaction was like, "Well, how about that. Never heard of such a thing." The more he understood that this was normal, the more he accepted his wife and learned to manage the change. I'm happy to report this couple is doing great today.

Like this rather clueless young man, many couples misunderstand basic male/female differences. Noticing and understanding physical differences is child's play, but understanding emotional and behavioral differences can be challenging. How many times have you heard statements like these?

- "She talks about the same problems over and over again."
- "He withdraws into his cocoon after a stressful day when he should talk to me about it. Instead, he shuts me out."
- "She loves to argue. After I've said something once, that should be it. I don't want to talk about it again. But she keeps repeating the same stuff over and over."
- "She talks about a problem over and over again but when I tell her how to fix it, she goes berserk!"

Let me give you a ridiculous little example. When I'm at the office, I drink water from a coffee mug. It's what I have. It's practical. It's a beverage container, so who cares?

Women do—at least the ones in my office. They say it weirds them out. They contend that coffee mugs are for coffee, not water.

I think they are weird.

They see etiquette, what's proper, what's fashionably acceptable. I see practical. I am thirsty. I need water. My mug holds water nicely. It's even got a handle. (If they don't leave me alone, I'll drink water out of my shoe, like I do when I'm fishing.)

Isn't it great how God made us different? Different, but not wrong.

• *Communication differences.* We really are designed differently. Not just physically but emotionally—and with different communication abilities and styles.

Most women I know are typically better communicators and can outargue their husbands. There are exceptions to this rule, but generally this is true.

When it comes to thinking on her feet, my wife is a pro. I can't outargue her or outtalk her. When she is upset, she spits out angry points, deftly wrapped in a lawyer's logic that I can't touch. After she's finished, I'm still saying stupid things like, "Uh, what?" or "Wait, give me a second," or "What did you just say?" Sometimes I just stand there slobbering all over myself with that deer-in-the-headlights look.

The analogy that comes to mind in these situations is that Rhonda is a Lamborghini, passing me at 95 mph on the freeway while I'm poking along in the slow lane like an old Chevy, doing the minimum speed limit. Some men may be better communicators with their wives when upset than others. I'm just not hardwired that way.

I can't compete with her when it comes to communicating on my feet during an argument. And I have learned through the years to try to show some restraint and listen, asking for some time to process what she just said and cool down a little. Not only does this give me a little time to think about what Rhonda said and what I will say in response, but it also gives my fight-or-flight mechanism time to come down from "red alert." After a while, I can come back to Rhonda and discuss the issue more logically.

I tell couples that one of the best things they can understand about each other is that when one of them says, "I need to think about that," believe it! It's probably true. Maybe he or she needs to process the 6,357 words you have just thrown on the table in the last 2.5 seconds. What you may interpret as stubbornness or indifference may really be a legitimate excuse.

If your spouse is a quick processor, you should likewise be patient when he or she processes gigabytes of information in a short period of time. Your spouse probably works things out by talking about it. You should accept and understand that he or she may have already arrived at a conclusion while you're still traveling to get there! Don't resent this difference or use it to berate your spouse. Just be accepting.

Like Rhonda and me, you and your spouse are likely very different when it comes to communication. Learn what those differences are, appreciate them, and develop new and healthier ways to communicate. (See chapter 8 for more discussion on communication and listening.)

• *Family influence.* Each one of us has learned behavior from our family of origin. We have unique memories, emotions, and yes, even genes.

A parent's genes influence a child's emotional, physical, and social architecture. Granted, we learn some behavioral or emotional tendencies, but some can be genetically influenced. If Dad tended to be quick on the trigger, in all likelihood Junior will be as well. If Mom struggled with depression, it's possible that Susie will too.

This isn't set in stone, but it's common to see personality types, certain illnesses, and similar behaviors running in families.

Genes are strong influencers. You can't wash them off or get a vaccination to rid yourself of their influence. Understanding and then accepting that your spouse may be influenced by genetics in how he or she thinks, believes, or acts may go a long way in preventing being hurt.

• *History.* Your mate's social experiences will affect your marriage.

If she grew up poor, that experience will affect her in various ways. He may tend to overachieve in order to rise above his past, or may save money more than the average person. She may spend money like a Hollywood starlet.

This doesn't mean you can blame unhealthy behavior on your upbringing. Just because your parents were thieves, does that give you a license to stuff your pockets at Target? No. Each person is responsible for his or her own actions.

But to make the assumption that the way you were raised—or that the environment or geographic area in which you were raised in—has nothing to do with how you think, feel, and behave?

Well, that's naïve at best. Without a doubt, your past affects your present.

• *Personality.* Are you a Lion, Beaver, Otter, or Golden Retriever? No matter what you are, your personality style is not wrong, just different. This applies to your spouse also. The bottom line is that none of us are the same. We all have different personalities. Because of this, we don't communicate the same; we have differing expectations, handle conflict distinctively, process stress uniquely, tackle problems in a particular way, and prefer various levels of social interaction.

Thank God we're different. If we were all alike, the world would be a mighty boring place. Differences keep life full of color and challenges. Our differences allow us to use various gifts and talents to resolve a variety of issues in our problem-filled world.

When you're born with a particular personality, your basic core traits cannot be easily changed. Some components of personality, however, can be adjusted. At least, temporarily. For example, some people who are introverted can become extroverted in short bursts. Because of job requirements, they may be able to stretch out like a rubber band for seven to eight hours. But when they get home, it's likely that they will snap back into shape, or their preferred personality style.

Mark worked at a marketing firm. Tracy was a homemaker. While Mark was at work, he interacted with many clients all day. His ability to be social and outgoing was vital to his success. When he arrived home in the evenings, his behavior changed. Mark is naturally an introvert, but for eight hours a day he could stretch himself to become extroverted. Unfortunately, by the time five o'clock rolled around, he was on people overload. His wife, Tracy, saw a "Marketing Mark" and a "Home Mark."

And she didn't much like living with the Home Mark.

As you might imagine, this caused serious problems in their marriage. Tracy asked her husband why he couldn't be as outgoing at home as he was at work. Mark really didn't have an answer, and the tension grew greater in their marriage.

At a couples retreat hosted by their church, Mark and Tracy learned that people can stretch outside their preferred personalities for a while for specific needs, but tend to revert to their natural style.

Once Tracy understood this principle, she stopped believing Mark was giving something at work that he refused to give at home, and her jealousy disappeared.

Understanding personality types really can lead to acceptance, and acceptance to healing.

GIVE WAY

On our twentieth anniversary, my wife and I found the ultimate vacation deal for underprivileged church workers. We flew out of Birmingham, Alabama, to the Bahamas for three days at $199.00 per person, round-trip air and hotel. Though we were at a Holiday Inn two miles from the beach, we thought we were in heaven.

Of the many positive things that occurred on that trip, one of the highlights for me was the "yield" signs. Okay, hear me out. Yield signs in the Bahamas look like ours here in the United States, except the wording is different. Instead of saying "Yield" they read, "Give way."

I was so struck with the sign that I took a photo of it. Even though I looked like a nut staring and taking a picture of a yield sign, it was an epiphany for me. I thought, *Man, giving way is the key to a lot of marriage problems today, mine included.*

Couples have to be willing to give way in every area possible. I know some couples that understand this concept well and others that never will. Learning to give way—even regarding the myth that "I can change my spouse"—is often a key breakthrough to a great marriage.

Isn't it interesting that so many of us walk into marriage seeing only our mate's strengths, but so many walk out of their marriage seeing only their faults?

It doesn't have to be that way with you.

Chapter Four

"I Didn't Marry My Soul Mate"

"LaFawnduh is the best thing

that has ever happened to me.

I'm 100 percent positive she's my soul mate."

—Kip Dynamite[1]

WHAT COULD COMPARE to *Gone with the Wind*, as Scarlett and Rhett proclaim their love, holding each other passionately as the theme music soars and a Southern sunset splashes the sky?

Well . . . there's *Napoleon Dynamite*.

In this '80s throwback comedy, Hollywood set a new standard for romance. It happened when a starry-eyed Kip Dynamite stretched his neck to look up into LaFawnduh's eyes (she was a least a foot and a half taller) and proclaimed her to be his soul mate.

I sat in the front row of the theater sniffling and wiping tears from my eyes. Not because my heart was touched by romantic splendor on the screen, but because I was laughing out of control. I have never witnessed a tackier (but funnier) love scene in my life. "I'm 100 percent positive she's my soul mate," Kip proudly asserted to his brother Napoleon. He spoke with such assurance, authority, and confidence.

As silly as the romance was between Kip and LaFawnduh, Hollywood has been stirring the soul mate pot for a long time in our culture, showing couples who are just destined to be together, despite all odds.

Now don't get me wrong. Everyone dreams of finding that person who seems to be "the one."

I remember distinctly talking to friends and my father about whether Rhonda was "the one." My gut feeling told me that she was the woman I had dreamed of most of my life. I felt pretty certain.

I still do.

THE YEARNING

The idea of a soul mate, at least the way the world sees it, is really misleading. As Christians we believe that God definitely brings His people together to fulfill a purpose. We all yearn for a mate who will connect to our "soul," a friend and partner to spend the rest of our life with.

The Bible touches on similar themes when it says that a man and woman should become "one," that a husband should honor his wife, and be willing to die for her (Ephesians 5:25–31). That is a level of intimacy, of souls touching, that God really wants.

And it's a process.

It's not so much a matter of finding "the one," as *becoming* one.

Oneness is not something you arrive at like checking into a retirement home—where you stay put until the good Lord calls you home. Oneness, intimacy, is something you build. It's an ongoing process that you must tend to with great care.

Pursue it, claim it, and reclaim it as often as necessary.

A soul mate is not something that you look for or find like an Easter egg or a missing wallet. *A soul mate is someone that you become.*

It is a process that takes place in marriage, over time. You don't start out there. There is no such thing as a mythological, astrologically driven nirvana that many people seem to be looking for today. This view of "soul mate-ism" basically trusts in the idea that there's only one person out there for me—that from the beginning of time there was one person selected for me and that I should search for that individual nonstop until I find him/her.

Some people believe that if two people are compatible, if they "match" on a variety of levels, then they have found The One. However, Dr. John Gottman, a leading marriage researcher, says that "similarity is, at best, a weak predictor of marital outcomes." He goes on to explain that similarity alone really doesn't provide insight into the processes that can maintain or destroy a marriage. Perceptions and beliefs about compatibility impact a marriage more than personality differences themselves.[2]

As a marriage counselor with numerous years of experience under my belt, I'm here to tell you there is a quality that's much more significant than compatibility: commitment.

Modern research also backs this up. Some of the nation's leading researchers say: "In most cases, a strong commitment to staying married not only helps couples avoid divorce, it helps more couples achieve a happier marriage."[3]

Commitment is about making a choice—and then sticking with it. A firm level of commitment positions all the other important pieces of marriage to fit together. As you work toward reaching that point, you become soul mates in the sense that you complete each other, you understand each other, you accept each other, and you avoid making quick judgments about each other without knowing the facts. Solid commitment in marriage provides the breathing room, experience, and connection for couples to join together in heart and soul over time.

This is the principle of committed love that Paul describes in 1 Corinthians 13:

A love that is patient and kind. A love that is neither prideful nor self-seeking. A love that can't easily be angered, and keeps no scorecard of past hurts. A love that always protects, never stops trusting, never gives up hope, and hangs in there for the long haul.

I'm not saying that compatibility doesn't help. Of course it does. I'm simply making the point that compatibility is not the most important thing in selecting a spouse—or deciding whether to keep that person or trade him or her in for a different model.

I can say without hesitation that my wife is my friend and soul mate in the sense that we are deeply connected to each other. But on our wedding day, I really didn't know that for sure. In fact, it took many years of living life together to get to this level of assurance.

And quite frankly, we're still in process.

There are days when we don't feel or act like soul mates. Even after twenty-six years, our soul mate barometer is affected by "the weather"—what's going on inside us and around us.

THE PRINCIPLE OF SHOWING UP

Nobody signs up for storms.

Nobody applies for hardships, or pencils in heartbreaks and setbacks into their calendar. We wish such dark days and sleepless nights would never enter our lives, descend upon our home, or challenge our marriage.

But they will anyway. If not today or tomorrow, then next week. It's a sure thing. That's part of life on a broken planet. Jesus said, "Here on earth you will have many trials and sorrows. But take heart, because I have overcome the world" (John 16:33 NLT).

God gave us marriage as a resource, a comfort, and a blessing to sustain us in these inevitable seasons of "trials and sorrows." And in His amazing wisdom and grace, He even worked it so that those rough patches in life could contribute to *strengthening* our marriage relationships.

When we walk through difficult times together, we are positioned to rise to a level of oneness that we could not experience any other way. Trials position us to become more like God. Our commitment gives us an unprecedented opportunity to complement each other, to draw from each other's strengths and wisdom, to compensate for the other's weaknesses and blind spots, to encourage each other, to be a coach, a friend, sexual partner, and to cover each other's backs and stand with each other when no one else will.

The hurtful realization that "my expectations are dashed to the ground by this person that I believed was my soul mate" may actually lead you to a good place in your relationship. When expectations are cut to the floor, the best response is not to leave them there to decompose but to pick them up and rebuild them with greater determination. Use your new, more realistic expectations to reenergize your marriage.

As we used to say growing up in a small surfing town in Florida, "When you get wiped out, grab your board and point it in the direction of the next big one." Another one I like is: "When you face a tidal wave—surf!"

And so if you went into your marriage thinking that this was your soul mate, and now all of a sudden things are really tough, I can understand how you might think you made a mistake. It may be that when you look into your spouse's face, he or she looks more like the son or daughter of Satan instead of a soul mate.

I often teach that part of being successful in marriage is *showing up*—being there emotionally and physically no matter how hurt or hopeless we feel. It sometimes comes down to showing up long enough to let the "stinking thinking," actions, and bad feelings subside until the good ones come back.

(Physical abuse is another issue. "Showing up" in an abusive situation could be very dangerous. Be wise and seek professional help immediately.)

I had a student stop me in a class on "Family Living for the Business Professional" one evening while I was talking about this principle. She was surprised by my comment, and said that I had offended her by saying there was such a thing as "just showing up" in a successful marriage.

"Surely you don't mean that! Who wants to just show up in a marriage where you are not happy anymore and all you do is argue?"

"Well, yes," I replied, "I do. That is exactly what I mean. I have observed in successful marriages that there is an element of showing up. I believe it's tied closely to ongoing, reinvested commitment. The deepest level of commitment says, 'I will be there even when I don't feel like it, act like it, or think like it.'

"It's almost a type of relational patriotism that says, 'I will stand for my wife or husband, no matter what. Even when it might be easier to abandon ship, I will stay and keep on trying. Even if it's not the politically correct thing to do. I have learned that no matter what my spouse does, I must keep showing up.'

"To me 'just showing up' implies there will be times when you have to stop worrying about what happened today, stop the argument, start fresh, and recommit to the process. There have been times in my job through the years when my performance wasn't strong, projects were stagnant, and everything seemed to be going in the wrong direction. It seemed as if I couldn't do anything right. But as frustrated and discouraged as I was, I kept showing up. And eventually things changed. Either I came up with a new idea, my mean supervisor was transferred, a few coworkers jumped in to help, or I simply changed my attitude. Showing up positioned me for the time when changes could occur. I didn't want to be there. I wasn't always excited to be there. But I kept showing up."

Now that I had their attention, I went on: "Research seems to lend some credence to this idea. In one study 86 percent of couples who were unhappy *but stuck it out* were happy five years later. The amazing thing about this was that these people didn't do anything huge or complicated to solve their problem. Many said that during this time some of the stressors that were causing tension simply went away. Problems such as financial slumps, kids in their teen years, in-law problems, illness, hurt feelings, and attitude issues were often resolved by one or both spouses, or the problem resolved itself. Many in this study didn't even go to counseling during this time period. They just kept showing up!"[4]

Several in my class that night just couldn't buy into this. They argued back and forth for ten or fifteen minutes until a student named Bo raised his hand: "I hear what you guys are saying, but I have to agree with Professor Temple. I am a personal testimony that 'showing up' works.

"Seven years ago my wife told me that she was in love with an officer in my flight squadron. She said she hadn't slept with him, but that it was probably going to happen because they cared deeply for each other. I thought that I had made the biggest mistake of my life in marrying her.

"Yet, after some time, even though my heart was ripped out, I decided that in spite of the way she felt, I wanted to fight for my marriage. I didn't start with her. I focused on me, on making changes inside that could make a difference.

"A couple of months later, after some incredible tough days and nights, we attended a church service together. After the service she told me she'd had a change of heart. She knew her feelings were wrong for this man. She realized that she had allowed feelings, which were intended only for me, to be given to him. She wanted that to change, for our marriage and for the kids' sake.

"It took some time, but she broke off all contact with this guy. She let me listen to the phone call. She then became accountable for all her phone calls and for every minute away from me. For the next three or four months in counseling, her emotions shifted away from him and back toward me. But it wasn't like a straight line back—it was more like an up and down thing.

"I became the person I should have been all along, so she would want me back. Each morning before I got out of bed, I prayed sincerely that God would shape me that day and give me the strength to just show up.

"He did and I did. Some days I showed up for the kids. Other days I was there because I didn't have a choice. We didn't make enough money to split up. There were times that my mother's words rang in my ears and became the reason I stayed: 'God don't like quitters.' At times it was because of my religious beliefs—I knew God didn't want us to divorce. Whatever seemed most important to me on any given day became an anchor that held me in my marriage.

"I am convinced that if I had constantly focused on how much my wife had hurt me, or how I felt about her unfaithfulness, I would have given up early on. I have to be honest; this was one of the most difficult times of my life. Yet by the grace of God, a great deal of counseling, education, and support from friends, we have reached the point where we are truly happy.

"We fell back in love with each other, just as we fell out. We are by no means perfect. I'm just grateful to the good Lord that she stayed long enough for her feelings to change . . . and that I just kept showing up."

Bo sat down. There wasn't a sound in the room.

To say the least, discussion was over for the evening. This man had validated what I have seen in my own marriage and in the marriages of hundreds of couples all over this nation. There is tremendous value in showing up.

If you'll allow me, I'd like to add to this thought with a very significant page out of our family history.

THROUGH THE FIRE

In the fifth year of our marriage, we were expecting our second child. Kevin, our firstborn, was healthy as a horse and about as active. We assumed that Hannah would be as well. Though we never said anything like this in so many words, both of us privately concluded that *couples who had babies with health problems didn't include us.* That happened to "other people."

How wrong we were.

On Hannah's six-week checkup, her pediatrician heard a click in her hips as he moved her legs up and down. He sent us immediately to the orthopedic specialist who ordered X-rays. The X-rays showed that Hannah was born with severely dislocated hips. The specialist put her in a Pavlic harness and sent us home to wait for possible surgery just as soon as the surgery schedule allowed.

"The sooner we address this," the doctor told us, "the higher the chances that Hannah's hips will develop properly."

Though optimistic, we were devastated. Yes, this problem was correctable, but like most young parents facing something like this, we feared the worse. *Surgery on our baby? A body cast for three months? This shouldn't be happening to us!* We cried ourselves to sleep together every night.

To add to this tough situation, within two weeks' time, my grandmother died unexpectedly, and my father, at age forty-seven, suffered a massive heart attack and endured a quadruple bypass.

"God! How much more can we take?" we asked over and over. "Why are You doing this to us?"

The only reply we heard for sure was complete, utter silence.

Nevertheless, the more we waited and the more we listened, the more we heard and understood. God spoke to us all the way through this crisis. He sent people to help us, to walk beside us, and to carry us. He even gave us the opportunity to help other young couples who were going through the same type of problems. We formed our own little "congenital hip displacement support group" in our city. God used our pain to ease the anxiety and distress of others.

Though the stress and pain took its toll on our marriage, it forged our hearts together in ways that nothing else could have done. There's no amount of book reading, marriage conferences, or counseling that could have shaped our marriage and hearts the way this period of our lives did. We became soul mates through the heat of that fire.

Twenty years later, we walked through the tragic accident and death of my only brother and close friend. It was the greatest tragedy our family had ever experienced. I can't imagine going through this tragedy with the degree of peace I did without Rhonda walking beside me. We connected deep into our souls during this extremely difficult time.

When you add up the sum total of happy, sad, daily living together, I can say we are soul mates—soul mates, indeed.

All of life is a learning process. When you stop learning, you really stop living. Yes, you might go on *breathing* after that, but you couldn't really call it "life." Marriage is a major part of that schooling. The more you learn, the more you realize how much there's left to know. And through all of the ups and downs, failures and successes, triumphs and heartaches . . . you are learning about life, you're learning about each other, and you're learning again and again about the grace and wisdom of God.

So, you show up, stick with it, pick yourself up after major stumbles, and keep walking down the road together.

That's how you become strong.

That's how you become soul mates.

Marriage is not the final destination. It is part of the process to help shape us and mold us for a better life.

Often the whole issue of thinking this "isn't my soul mate" has to do more with our frame of mind, with our attitude, our thinking. If I go back and look at what I expected of my wife before marriage, I realize now that *nobody* could have fulfilled them. Put together any combination you like—Mother Teresa, Joan of Arc, Cleopatra, Marilyn Monroe—no woman could have attained to such stratospheric expectations. Disappointment (of course) was inevitable. I survived those deflated expectations, licked my wounds, and made up my mind to discover my soul mate . . . and to become one.

Knowing what I know about Rhonda today, without hesitation, I would choose her all over again. If someone asked me to choose between thousands of beautiful women in a long line with the greatest display of physical, intellectual, and spiritual qualities, I would choose Rhonda. Her beauty goes deeper than anyone's. I want to walk through the gates of heaven hand in hand with this woman. She is the most beautiful creature in the universe to me, inside and out.

I believe that, and I remind myself of that belief day after day. When my thoughts and emotions begin to pull me away from that lofty place, I line 'em back up again. I know that Rhonda feels similarly about me. (Especially the "most beautiful man in the world" part.)

But how did we get to this point?

There's no supermagical formula. There's no fifteen-step program you order from a 1-800 number on cable TV. It is just living life, sometimes joyfully, sometimes with regret, but learning to live it *together* with God in our hearts.

Sam and Sugar

LET ME SHARE A SWEET STORY WITH YOU. It's the story of my good friend Sam and his wife, Mildred, affectionately referred to by friends as "Sugar."

Sam and Sugar began their lives together while Big Band music filled the air, almost seventy years ago. Sam hired me over seventeen years ago as he served as an elder of a large church in Alabama. Though our worlds were separated by over forty years, we became the finest of friends. Sam became a spiritual, vocational, and even marital mentor to me. Through the years, I carefully watched how Sam and Sugar loved each other at a deep and rare level.

I also had the honor of walking with them through some of the most difficult chapters in their life. I was at the hospital when the doctor told Sam that Sugar might not make it through her illness. She was in the hospital for weeks, attached to wires, tubes, monitors, and respirators. We prayed and prayed together, asking the gracious Father to give them just a little more time together.

The Lord granted us our petitions. Sam and Sugar have weathered numerous storms together since then, and they're still together.

Once when we were talking over a cup of coffee, Sam spoke of the darkest, loneliest memory he'd ever had. It took place at about four in the morning, in the dead of winter, as he was leaving for the German front during World War II. With tears in his eyes, Sam recalled looking back through the window of a passenger train, through the clouds of smoke thrown up by the steam engine, to see Sugar crying, holding their three-year-old son. He said he would never forget seeing his family fade into the darkness behind him as he journeyed toward two of the most horrific years of his life.

Neither Sam nor Sugar knew if they would ever hold each other again. Sam's heart ached and yearned all the way through the war. The only personal items he was able to hold onto throughout the entire campaign were a picture of his family, a New Testament, a toothbrush, and a bloodstained dollar bill.

Though Sam wanted to return to his wife and son, he was also a man of extraordinary patriotism. Once, as Sam's platoon neared a darkened beachhead, German forces unleashed a barrage of fire. Sam's comrades and friends were falling all around. The amphibious duck (armored sea vehicle) they were in was ankle-deep in blood. The cries of the dying were as loud or louder than the artillery.

Though Sam's picture of Sugar and his son were warm to his heart and ever before his mind, he jumped into the water grabbing a mounted machine gun. Sam began firing the weapon while walking straight into the oncoming fire screaming from a German bunker. Sam felt that if someone didn't do something, his entire group would be wiped out.

Because of Sam's unwavering courage, he was able to destroy the bunker single-handedly. The lull in enemy fire allowed the American forces to land onshore and eventually destroy and capture the enemy army. Many years later Sam was honored with the Bronze Star for his bravery.

My friend was a war hero. A real, live hero. But Sam was just as great a hero to me because of his faith and family life.

Sam and Sugar are the epitome of soul mates. For almost three-quarters of a century, they have been loving each other unconditionally through the storms and valleys of life. Both almost ninety years old, they move slower and with more care than they did years ago.

But they still kiss before they go to sleep.

They still go to worship together almost every Sunday.

And they still hold hands.

It is what the hand-holding represents that keeps Sam and Sugar together: oneness. Unwavering oneness.

I recently received an e-mail from Sam. In answer to a question I asked him about Sugar, he said, "Sugar is my soul mate. The choices we made together are what forged our souls. We are at the point in our life where we thank God before we climb out of bed together each day that He has graciously given us one more day to enjoy being together. After our thanks, we humbly ask Him for one more day together. Though we yearn for heaven, we love each other so much that we want to hang out just one more day. We really are each other's best friends. We are what Jesus asked us to be . . . one.

"No, we are not perfect. I still get on Sugar's nerves a lot, especially when I can't hear what she says. We still have an argument here and there, but neither of us has enough energy to finish it. But we are one.

I believe that God is preparing us each day He gives us together for our journey through eternity together."

Now, that's a marriage worth working for, don't you agree? Don't let the myth "I made a mistake—I didn't marry my soul mate" rob you of it.

Chapter Five

"My Needs Come First"

"Marriage is not just spiritual communion,

it is also remembering to take out the trash."

—Dr. Joyce Brothers[1]

I REMEMBER THE EASTER SUNDAY years ago when our family went to visit at the home of some church folks.

My brother and I were in our Easter best: new white polyester slacks, purple shirts, white patent leather slip-ons, and ties that I remember being as wide as our bodies. To a couple of ten- and eleven-year-old country boys, our Easter outfits were like a four-lane highway: fast and loud.

The last thing Mom said to us when we got out of our blue '67 Ford was: "Don't get dirty! You will not live to see twelve if either of you ruin your new clothes!"

We headed out across the backyard of our friends, Sam and Jake. They were whistling and motioning, perched up on the split rail fence around the pig lot. (You know where this is going, don't you?)

Jake courageously mounted the meanest, ugliest, fattest, dirtiest pig in the pen. Gripping the poor pig's right ear with one hand, he lifted the other high in the air, rodeo style. To the loud shrieks and squeals of pig and spectators alike, he rode out his eight seconds like a pro, triumphantly dismounted, and stood in the middle of the pen. Like a gladiator with his hands on his hips, he boldly issued the ultimate testosterone challenge: "Who can beat that?"

I immediately looked at my brother. He looked at me. With the skill of a bronco rider, Brad jumped on the back of the pig and rode him around the pen several times. Since my brother was obviously successful and didn't seem to mess his pants up (especially since we only looked at the front side), I decided there was no way on earth that I was going to let those guys show me up.

I shot down into the muddy pen, mounted the hog, knowing that my ride had to be *better* than theirs.

So, I sat on the pig backward.

Right from the start, I realized that I had chosen a much more complex maneuver. No sooner had I climbed on the big fellow than he rose up on his back legs and sent me straight into the black, gooey mud. Every inch of my little body was covered. The smell burned my nose. But hey, sweet, sweet pain.

We rode pigs without shame or consciousness for about two hours—two of the best hours of my entire life. Sweet pleasure indeed, until we heard Dad's "it's time to go" whistle.

I will never forget the look on Mom's face as she saw us heading toward her. Her face was the most ruby red I ever remember seeing it. That's all I remember. I must have blacked out. My brother and I cried most of the way home that day, nursing our pain—pain caused by our own selfish desire to be like our buddies.

Kids are like that. They are selfish by nature. One of the first words kids learn is "mine!" which, by interpretation, means "I want this because I am selfish, and I want to do whatever I want to do."

As we marry, we make some of the same selfish demands that we did as children. We just use different terms. "You always want it *your* way, don't you?" or "I never get to do what *I* want," and on and on.

Sometimes we do things we know very well will displease others, but all we can think about is how great the satisfaction and outcome will be for us. It's the "what's in it for me" dynamic. Like a computer program, this mentality runs in the background of our psyches for most of our lives.

The mud washed off that Easter Sunday almost thirty-five years ago, but the selfishness didn't. When I married Rhonda, she knew she had her hands full when one day during an argument, I looked her square in the eyes and said, "Right now I could care less about what *you* want!"

I don't know what I was expecting for an answer to a statement like that, but what my wounded bride actually said was, "Get out and don't come back."

So, I got out. And I didn't come back . . . for a while. After a brief solo journey on the road, considering the future of living alone, no companionship (and no home cooking), I decided to repent.

I confessed my selfishness and swallowed my pride.

I've become very proficient at those things. It's a frame of mind I've needed frequently throughout my marriage career.

MILE-HIGH EXPECTATIONS

Selfishness also creeps into marriage in the form of expectations.

Remember high school track meets? I always like watching the high jump, where they kept raising the bar higher and higher until no one can clear it anymore. But you don't start out at the school record mark and expect kids to "measure up."

You can't do that in marriage, either. When your expectations are a mile high in marriage, how do you expect your spouse to ever clear the bar? Holding unrealistic expectations of a spouse because of your own selfish desires will only increase the distance between the ground (reality) and the bar you set (expectations). This will guarantee greater disappointment in your marriage.

For example, if one of a wife's expectations is that her husband will be exactly like he was when they were dating, she has set the bar too high. He was probably like most guys, running on testosterone and very affectionate. He may never be like he was when dating, but if he were coached or taught properly, he might be able to become a more passionate and caring person.

If a husband clings to the expectation that his wife will join him every weekend for fishing trips or sporting activities, he's setting the bar too high. She may not be able to muster the will to go every weekend. But she might be able to accompany him on a hiking excursion or day at the golf course occasionally.

Marriage is all about adjusting our expectations—*and doing so regularly.*

Hurt, disappointment, and frustration result when there is a wide gap between what we expect (expectations) and what actually happens (reality). The closer we can get our expectations to line up with the truth, the less hurt we will experience.

The key is to check those cherished expectations of ours under the cold hard light of truth/reality. "Is this even reasonable? Am I being realistic? Are these things really attainable? Are they attainable for my spouse? Do these expectations make sense under our current circumstances?" Questions like these help to bring us out of the clouds and back to earth again.

WHEN "RIGHTS" ARE WRONG

Expectations aren't the only thing we need to realign in marriage. Often we also have to wrestle with the issue of rights.

Would you like to know one of the single most powerful, effective, and life-changing choices you could ever make in your marriage? Are you ready for this?

It is the conscious, ongoing, sometimes daily decision to give up rights.

Getting married means giving up the life of a single-person mind-set. Married people have to learn to think in terms of being one, which happens to involve another person. It is a team mind-set, no longer an individual one.

I've never put much stock in trends, but when it comes to my marriage counseling, I've certainly observed one that disturbs me. It is the tendency in Christian marriages to displace what God wants in our lives with the desire to "have my own needs met."

I see that as a problem. It's a problem when my way is more important than letting God have His way. The culture has apparently influenced us more than we realize. Satan has slipped another unhealthy myth into our hearts.

Look at what God's Word says about the need to "give up" certain things in order for relationships to flourish:

> Let nothing be done through selfish ambition or conceit, but in lowliness of mind let each esteem others better than himself. Let each of you look out not only for his own interests, but also for the interests of others. Let this mind be in you which was also in Christ Jesus, who, being in the form of God, did not consider it robbery to be equal with God, but made Himself of no reputation, taking the form of a bondservant, and coming in the likeness of men. And being found in appearance as a man, He humbled Himself and became obedient to the point of death, even the death of the cross. (Philippians 2:3–8 NKJV)

The Scriptures are pretty plain: Don't allow selfishness to ruin your life or your relationships. Period.

Dr. Bill Doherty, a friend and colleague, is one of the most knowledgeable marriage researchers in the country. He feels that besides issues like excessive busyness, career-first mind-sets, media influence, reduced intimacy, less connection, and less focus on relationships in general, one of the main threats to marriage today is a "consumer mind-set."

Dr. Doherty puts it like this:

> The consumer attitude toward marriage is all around us and affects all of us, like air pollution. We can detect it most readily when we are bothered by something in our mate or our marriage and hear ourselves thinking or saying things like, "What am I getting out of this marriage, anyway?" or "I deserve better" or "What's in this for me?" Not that these thoughts are altogether inappropriate; if your spouse is having an affair or hitting you, then focusing on self-interest is quite appropriate. But when your mate is not the lover you had hoped for, or nags you more than you

want, or is not emotionally expressive enough for you, then consumer thinking suggests that you have not cut the best possible deal in marrying this person. Then you start to do cost-benefit analysis: what am I getting from this relationship in terms of what I am putting into it?[2]

Dr. Scott Stanley and other leading marriage researchers are also seeing similar findings.[3] Real sacrifice is the deliberate choice of giving something up for the sake of another. Marriages that do best are the ones in which two people decide daily to give up and to sacrifice for the other. It's a strong predictor of marital success and longevity. Ongoing selfishness is a strong predictor of divorce.

Dr. Doherty adds this line of thinking: "You can work your way out of a reasonably good marriage by focusing on what you are not getting out of it and turning negative toward your mate, who will in turn give you even less and thereby help justify your leaving."[4]

ARE YOU A MARRIAGE "CONSUMER"?

One of the things Rhonda and I try to do with couples at marriage seminars is challenge their thinking, helping them to replace their flawed reasoning with healthier thoughts. Once a couple sees how flawed their thinking has become and how it is destroying their marriage, they become teachable. They begin to look at things differently. They typically begin to see the bigger picture.

Here are some indicators that you are being influenced by the consumer mind-set myth, the incredibly destructive fantasy that says "Marriage is all about meeting my needs."

- I see only what I am not getting out of marriage.
- My focus is on why my mate is not meeting my needs.
- I fail to see my own weaknesses, but continually highlight my spouse's.

- I compare my marriage to "the couple at church," to the people next door, or to my coworkers.
- I believe that what I want is the same as what I need.
- I feel that I deserve better and should be treated better.
- I make demands of my spouse that I am not willing to apply to myself.
- My expectations and fantasies drive whether I engage or not engage, serve or not serve, stay or not stay.[5]

The 2007 State of the Union report conducted by Rutgers University puts marriage trends in America under the microscope. One section of the report discusses the growing decline in favorableness toward marriage. The report suggests that cohabitation is growing at an unprecedented rate and marriage trends seem to be moving away from traditional views and practices.

The authors seem to attribute this phenomenon to a couple of factors. One is a gradual abandonment of religious attendance and beliefs, and another is a growing acceptance of "expressive values" that preclude a preoccupation with personal autonomy and self-fullfillment.[6]

THE PROBLEM WITH BEIGE

Try this experiment: Look around the room and locate three objects that are beige in color. Have you found them? Now, try to recall one object that is the color green. Notice what you may have had to do. You had to look again and search a second time for the green object. Why? You were so focused on beige objects that you ignored all others.

In marriage, when we become self-centered, we only see "beige." That's the reason the Rutgers report makes so much sense. It establishes that we are having a breakdown in family, marriage, and society not only because people's values are becoming broader and more accepting of other beliefs (less focused on God's truth), but also because people in general are becoming more self-centered.

I have a close friend who often jokes: "Yeah, Mitch old boy, it's all about me! God carries a group picture of me in His wallet." Well, most people are not that extreme, but honestly I have worked with some who come pretty close.

Each of us has both a giving and taking side, but when one or the other predominates long-term, it causes problems. Takers take advantage of people who care about them; givers are taken advantage of. With takers, the discussion and spotlight seems always to come back to them—their needs, their rights, and their preferences. Maybe at some point they see light shades of other colors around them, but mostly they see "beige." In other words they're looking through distorted lenses, and all they see is "me."

When you become "beige," others will hear it in your conversation. And frankly, it sounds more than a little like whining.

"You never consider me first" . . . "I went first last time" . . . "You never say you're sorry" . . . "You never give enough to me" . . . "You always think of yourself first" . . . "I have rights too" . . . "I need space" . . . "I need to focus on me for a while."

Please understand, some of these are legitimate complaints. We all need affection, companionship, intimacy, commitment, and attention. I have seen husbands and wives who had every right to speak up and complain because they were being neglected and mistreated by their spouse.

Even so, a consistent focus on myself and my needs and wants has a way of removing my ability to see the "colors of life." When people worship needs, particularly our own, we become beige and can't see anything or anyone else.

LESSONS FROM THE GOOD SAMARITAN

If you have ever darkened the door of a Sunday school room, you've heard the story. Luke chapter 10 tells the story of a man who unexpectedly sacrificed his own rights to rescue someone who would have never expected his help.

Most of us know it as Jesus' parable of the good Samaritan.

A man on the road to Jericho was attacked, beaten, robbed, and left for dead by the side of the road. Two different religious officials—a priest and a Levite—chose not to "become involved." They passed by and did not help the injured man. Then a Samaritan, despised by the Jews, came across the man and stopped to help.

This story has such great application for marriage.

1. *The Good Samaritan was more interested in serving than being served.*

The priest and Levite were religious leaders, but they lacked a compassionate heart. They were looking through myopic, self-centered eyes. They seemed to be driven by the myth "It is all about me, my welfare, my comfort, my schedule, and the way that other religious people perceive me." They determined it was too risky to help this man.

The scorned Samaritan, however, saw the man, wounded and barely conscious, and wasted no time in helping him.

Hmm, how often have I done the same thing when I saw that my wife was deeply hurting?

One of the great truths of this story is the fact that being "religious" does not necessarily instill in a person righteous attitudes and actions. The truth is we must overcome our selfish nature and develop an eye to help, sacrifice, and serve at any given moment—especially our own mates.

2. *The Samaritan was intentional about his compassion.*

The text says that the Samaritan "took pity" on the wounded man (v. 33). In other words, the Samaritan was intentionally empathetic toward that wounded crime victim. Though he may have experienced a brief moment of fear, he overcame with a stronger, deeper core principle—compassion.

I once asked a large group of couples at a marriage retreat to tell me what kept them from serving their spouse, as they knew they should. Can you guess the number one answer?

It was *fear*.

The most common fears were: (1) fear of doing the wrong thing, (2) fear of making matters worse, (3) fear of saying things that would embarrass me, (4) fear of being rejected, and (5) the fear of being used.

Developing a spirit of compassion and empathy will overcome any fear of serving another. Compassion is more powerful than fear. It will cause a husband or wife who has hurt the other to say, "I am sorry. Will you please forgive me?" even when he or she is not convinced it was all his or her fault.

3. *The Samaritan put his concern into action.*

"He . . . bandaged his wounds, pouring on oil and wine" (v. 34). The Samaritan could have offered excuses . . . he wasn't prepared, it wasn't his affair, or he didn't have time. Instead, he simply used the supplies and time in front of him. In that day wine was used as an anesthetic, and oil was used to soothe wounds and ease pain.

When you are presented the opportunity to serve your spouse, it will usually be at an inopportune time, or a time when you're least prepared. You can always make excuses as to why you shouldn't help: "This is a bad time for me" or "I was asked to work another shift."

No matter how inconvenient the opportunity may be, when it comes to marriage, action should take precedence over justification. Trust is built in a marriage when partners serve each other as the opportunity arises.

4. *The Samaritan was willing to be inconvenienced.*

"He put the man on his own donkey, took him to an inn and took care of him" (v. 34). The Samaritan could have reasoned that he didn't want to take the risk of becoming involved. He could have also reasoned from a social concern: "What if a friend or business associate sees me helping this man? He's different than I am. If I help him, my colleagues may look down on me. This could hurt my business."

Jesus referred to this man as "good" for a reason. He was willing to risk social status, safety, and even loss of business to serve. He did not allow inconvenience or fear to prevent him from helping.

Shouldn't we be just as willing to do the same for the wife of our youth or for the husband who was sent as a gift from God Himself?

I have to remember that it's often the little, everyday, seemingly unheroic things that I do for Rhonda that cause her to respect me and want to be closer to me. Cleaning up my mess on the kitchen table, putting up the laptop after I write, opening the door for her, sending flowers when she's had a bad day, calling her from work. She doesn't see me as a hero just because I do the big things like not forgetting birthdays or changing her flat tires. It's my duty to do the "big" things like that. But it's the little, daily, unexpected acts that I often have to make myself do that promote me to hero status in her mind.

Daily, little "Samaritan" actions are what build closeness, intimacy, and even more commitment in marriage.

I once asked an old blind preacher friend of mine, Brother Allen, what he felt was the key to success in marriage. He smiled at me, opened the back of his Bible, and pulled out a Braille sermon outline he had just preached the week before and held it in his hand.

From memory, he gave me the bottom line.

"*Serve* your wife like it's the last day God has given you on earth. It might just be your last. Don't waste it."

I couldn't have said it better.

DIGGING DITCHES IN MARRIAGE

In the Old Testament book of 2 Kings, chapter 3, we encounter the armies of three kings who were dying because they had no water. With all their strength, ingenuity, and preparation, neither the armies nor the kings could find a solution. They were in trouble and didn't know what to do. In fact, the king of Israel asked, "Has the Lord called us three kings together only to hand us over to Moab?" (v. 10).

To test their faith, God commanded the people, through the prophet Elisha, to simply start digging ditches. In desperation, they obeyed the illogical decree and dug trenches in the arid soil. Without a noisy show of blowing winds or rolling clouds, the ditches began to fill up. In fact, the entire valley became saturated with fresh water. The people were saved, kings and armies rejoiced, and God's people could go forward to face the challenges that lay ahead.

In our walk with God, in our daily lives, in marriage, we face relentless challenges. At times, our emotions tell us the situation is unsolvable. On one level, those fears are founded in truth. On our own, we truly *can't* solve the problem. The ground is too dry, the sky is too clear. No one has any ideas, and the situation doesn't look promising. But when we tap into God's power, the possibilities can rise up. Solutions can mysteriously climb to the top and lavishly bathe our problems in tranquility.

Just as thirst challenged the strongest of armies in a destitute land, so problems, trials, and seemingly insoluble concerns will darken the strongest of Christian marriages.

Are you struggling because your marriage seems hopeless? Do you wonder, as the king of Israel did, if God brought the two of you together just to watch you suffer? Do you feel neglected because your needs aren't being met?

Maybe you've tried reading every marriage book you can get your hands on. Possibly, you have become a seminar junkie. Maybe you've tried more than a few counselors to no avail. You've done all you know to do, and there seems to be no resolution. Your pain is profound and demoralizing.

Here's the question of the day: *Have you dug ditches in your marriage?* Have you fallen to your knees and asked God to meet the desires you cannot meet yourself? Have you been willing to let go and stop attempting to fix the problem on your own?

I have found that it is in the dry, arid, thirsty valleys of life where God does His greatest wonders and miracles. His marvelous works blow my mind when I humble myself and dig ditches.

Sure, books, seminars, and counseling can help almost any marriage. I'm a believer in these helps. But instead of conventional methods, maybe God is calling you to clear the path for Him to work the miracle.

It is usually when I respond to God's call to dig deeper in my own soul that He moves me out of the way and positions my life and marriage for radical transformation. It is at this point that God's grace rises up and fills my life with rushing streams of goodness.

Could it be possible that God is waiting on you to dig a ditch before He provides the miracle? Put your mind to it and remember that marriage is about so much more than meeting your needs.

Chapter Six

"Happiness Is Everything"

"I don't know what your destiny will be,
but one thing I do know: the only ones
among you who will be really happy are those
who have sought and found how to serve."

—Albert Schweitzer[1]

MARKETING EXECUTIVES ARE pretty smart people . . . at least for about fifteen seconds.

Back in the nineteenth century, it was the elixir salesmen and snake-oil hawkers who sold their patent medicine concoctions to people who genuinely wanted to feel better and were frightened by deteriorating health conditions.

Here are a few actual examples: There was *Dr. Bonkers Celebrated Egyptian Oil*, advertised to be effective for colic, cramps in the stomach, and cholera—in humans as well as horses and cattle. *Dr. Lindley's Epilepsy Remedy* promised to treat epilepsy, fits, spasms, convulsions, and St. Vitus's dance. *Dr. Mixer's World Renowned Blood Purifier* was billed as a remedy specially formulated to treat cancer, tumors, abscesses, ulcers, piles, rheumatism, and all blood disorders. *Dr. Solomon's Cordial Balm of Gilead* claimed to cure almost anything, but was particularly effective with venereal complaints. "Dr." Sibley, an English patent medicine seller of the eighteenth and early nineteenth centuries, even went so far as to claim that his *Reanimating Solar Tincture* would (as the name implies) "restore life in the event of sudden death."

Handy stuff to have around, right?

Right here in the twenty-first century, the claims of advertisers are more subtle and sophisticated, but—when you think about it, no less outlandish. Will wearing a particular brand of jeans really make me catch the eye of the opposite sex? Will driving a particular car make me feel powerful and sophisticated? Will a lady putting a particular cream on her face at night really look years younger?

Today's marketing firms may not be cure-alls in a corked bottle, but they still want us to believe that "if you buy our goods or service, your happiness button will be turned on forever."

Advertisers urge, "Swipe the card and you will experience incredible memories that will last forever" or "Pay four hundred bucks for two tickets to the Yankees game, and you and your son will be bonded for a lifetime." Pictures fade in and out on your TV screen, with smooth violins playing in the background. The ads almost make you cry (or throw up). What the advertisers don't tell you is that you will have to pay all these "memories" back with 21 percent interest.

It seems to me that most earthly promises of perpetual happiness are pretty empty and very likely short-term. I think that all media ads should carry the caution: "Warning: scientific research has proven that this product will increase or engage your emotions for only thirty minutes or less, if at all, and will not contribute to your ongoing happiness."

But the simple fact is . . . happiness sells.

Everybody wants it, rich or poor, young or old, male or female, so why not sell to it?

In a fifteen-year study published in the March issue of the *Journal of Personality and Social Psychology*, researchers found that people who were already satisfied with their lives before marriage were more likely to stay married longer. "While long-term marriages tend to be happy, a constant search for marital jubilation could be disastrous," said David Popenoe, codirector of the National Marriage Project. He continued, "It may be that one reason for divorce is they are looking to maintain that high level of happiness throughout the marriage, which is kind of impossible for most people."[2]

Well said, Dr. Popenoe.

At one time or another, we have all bought into the myth that some change in our circumstances—getting married, having a child, getting a divorce, moving across the country—will bring lasting happiness into our lives. But the simple fact is, if you weren't happy before this change, chances are pretty good you won't be happy afterward, either.

NO SUCH THING AS A HAPPY PILL

We Americans are "microwave consumers." We want it easy, and we want it fast. From our fast foods to automatic soap dispensers, we have it made. This "fast 'n' easy" mind-set spills over into our daily attitudes and relationships. We buy into myths such as, "I deserve to be happy in my marriage" or "This is not worth it" or "Happiness is the most important thing."

We want a happy pill for marriage. I have had clients actually say they are looking for one. If only there was such a pill. (I would become a pharmaceutical salesman today.) We look for it in books, seminars, and even lovers. It just doesn't exist.

As we go through the journey of marriage, living, loving, and learning, we experience happiness along the way. Joy becomes an umbrella under which we live. But it isn't the air we breathe every day. Happiness is a by-product of *right* living, not "easy living." And it's a life journey that will have ups and downs, highs and lows, and hits and misses along the way.

Alone in a cold prison cell toward the end of his life, the apostle Paul wrote: "I have learned to be content whatever the circumstances" (Philippians 4:11). Notice something. Paul said that contentment, a first cousin of happiness, was something he had *learned*.

It wasn't an elusive butterfly flitting down out of the clouds and alighting on top of his head. It was an intentional work in process. Not a pill. Even with direct endowment by God's Holy Spirit, Paul didn't find the pill. He cultured contentment and achieved it, even in a dungeon with chains on his ankles. The secret to Paul's success? He set his heart and his daily thoughts on the right things, and in turn, the right feelings and actions followed suit.

For over two thousand years, Paul's letter to the Philippian church that I quoted above has been known as "the epistle of joy." And it was written from a prison cell. That's what makes his statement "I have learned to be content" so incredibly powerful.

The principle holds true for a marriage too.

I believe that God did not simply give us marriage to repopulate the world, have a divinely approved outlet for sex, and to be happy. Sure, each of these things is important. But I think we sometimes forget that marriage truly is something very sacred. It has a much higher purpose than most of us consider or realize.

While Scripture has a great deal to say about couples being holy, it doesn't have a lot to say about us being all that happy. Even Christian marriages won't be happy all the time. God seems more concerned about right living than happy feelings.

When Christian couples become obsessed with chasing after non-happiness, they displace energy. Their energy goes into focusing on and pursuing things that create happiness, rather than focusing on and pursuing their Creator and one another.

In the early years of my marriage, the "I should be happy all the time" era, I looked for greener grass—not in the sense of infidelity but rather in constantly seeking approval from others. This search, I am embarrassed to say, became my mistress. I guess I didn't get all the acceptance and approval I craved as I was growing up, so I seemed to run on empty most of my life. I looked for it everywhere other than where I should.

One day while accompanying an old friend on a hospital visit, he turned to me and said, "Mitch, your identity is in Christ. Don't look for it in other places other than the places God ordained. You're not going to find happiness and identity in what others think about you. Stop depending on getting your affirmation from people. That's not the right source."

I felt like a spanked baby. But he was right.

The obsessive, fanatical pursuit of happiness, within or without marriage, will leave you tired, frustrated, and invariably disillusioned. It will create gaps between you and your spouse, not bridges.

THE TRUTH WILL MAKE YOU FREE (AND MAYBE MISERABLE)

Jesus said, "You will know the truth, and the truth will set you free" (John 8:32).

I believe that, of course. But when it comes to the practical side of family and marriage, I often say: "The truth will definitely set you free—but in the meantime, it might make you pretty miserable."

What I mean by that is that while truth can be excruciatingly painful, in the *long* run it really does provide freedom—freedom from unnecessary pain, suffering, conflict, and mistakes.

Following the path of right living, truth will provide freedom for everyone around you. As long as you follow the truth, God's basic principles for marriage and for life, you will not stumble around in the darkness. You will prove in practice the truth of the psalmist's words: "Your word is a lamp to my feet and a light for my path" (Psalm 119:105).

When I seek the Scriptures for guidance, in life, family, in marriage, I always do much better. I see happy days again, at least more often. It's when I start buying into ambiguous myths and lies fueled by selfishness that I miss joy. I can't blame that on my wife or anyone else. I must accept full responsibility.

Happiness is a good thing. God likes it. He made it up. One of the reasons He created us was for His pleasure (Revelation 4:11 KJV).

HAPPINESS GONE HAYWIRE

In marriage today it is common for us to seek freedom and fulfillment in everything imaginable—keeping up with the Joneses, power, money, rampant sex, romance novels, pornography, in-laws, and friends.

These are things that will give us a pathetic return for our investment. I tell people, "It's crazy for us to ruin our marriage trying to keep up with the Joneses; you don't know them anyway."

Here's a big truth I wish I had learned about twenty years earlier: When you chase happiness, you'll rarely catch up to it. But when you set your heart to live for God and follow the precepts and principles of His Word, happiness will sneak up on you and overtake you. In other words, it is a by-product of right living, not an end in itself.

Couples caught up in the happiness myth say, "As long as we're happy, that's the most important thing" or "Nothing else matters except that we are happy" or "All I want is to be happy."

Here's the skinny: It's not wrong to be happy, as long as we keep happiness in the proper perspective. The Scriptures mention joy over and over again, even commanding us to be joyful during trials. Happy people are healthy people. Healthy people are happy people (Proverbs 15:13). It works both ways.

Happiness comes naturally when couples put first things first.

The untainted truth that sets couples free to grow is this: *Marriage is more about serving and giving than happiness.*

Marriage is a place to put our mate's spiritual and eternal well-being above everything else. It's a place where we are to serve no matter what the other does or doesn't do. It's a place where God intends for us to stick it out no matter how dissatisfied we become. It's a place where God expects us to reflect His image to our children and to the world. Marriage, really, is more of a vehicle through which God shows us His purposes and righteousness rather then a means of simply making us happy all the time.

Couples who buy into the myth that happiness is more important than anything else in marriage are destined for frequent reality checks.

I don't mean to make marriage sound like a turnoff or a too-hard-to-achieve proposition. There is an incredible amount of happiness in marriage. After twenty-six years of marriage, I can honestly say I am happier than I have ever been in my life. Marriage is the most complete and incredibly satisfying relationship between two people who completely offer themselves to the other. And it's great fun.

But don't look for happiness in the wrong places because you're not getting it at home. It may just be time to make a few attitude and behavior adjustments in your own heart. If you are not happy in this marriage, you are not likely to be happy in another. The grass is never really greener on the other side. *The grass is greenest in the yard where you water it the most.* Make sure your daily thoughts, passions, and energy are spent on making your own lawn greener.

FORGIVENESS: NOT A ONETIME ACT

Are we still talking happiness here?

Then let me make this simple observation: Couples who learn how to forgive experience the happiness that some people search for all their lives. When I talk to couples that don't seem to be able to forgive, even after an appropriate time of healing has passed since they were offended, I try to find out why. I start asking questions. As I do, I usually see some lights come on.

1. *"Why are you afraid to forgive?"*

It's very common for couples to quickly answer this question with, "We're not afraid."

Well maybe, and maybe not. Typically fear *does* drive not being able to forgive. Some are afraid that if they forgive, they are in some way endorsing or approving what their spouse did. I remind them that Jesus forgave constantly while on earth without endorsing sin (John 4).

Some are afraid they will have to forget. No matter what has happened or how penitent your spouse is, you can't completely forget unless you have a lobotomy or get hit on the head really hard. God doesn't necessarily want or expect us to completely forget things that hurt us. Memories protect us. He simply wants us to let go of the anger, bitterness, and coldness we feel when we do not forgive.

Some are afraid of what they may have to give up. But what do you really lose if you forgive someone? The right to keep on punishing the other? The right to maintain power or control? The right to keep the other person in prison?

2. *Do you equate trust with forgiveness?*

I think so many couples can't forgive each other because they misunderstand the difference between forgiveness and trust. Forgiveness is more than a onetime act; it's a process. It begins with a decision to forgive but involves a process that often demands a great deal of work and energy in getting over the hurt. Jesus said to forgive infinitely, as much as necessary, even daily (Matthew 18:21–22). Just because you don't trust your spouse doesn't mean you can't forgive him or her. We can forgive people who commit murder and steal, but that doesn't mean we let our daughters go out with them or allow them to manage our bank account. Forgiveness can be given. Trust must be built, one brick, one action at a time. It may take years to rebuild trust when a spouse has been unfaithful, but forgiveness can happen much sooner.

As with "forgiveness," *grace* is a word that rolls quickly and easily off the tongue. Even so, it may be difficult to comprehend, to receive, or to give to others.

In marriage, I think traits like forgiveness and grace are more difficult and complicated than in other contexts.

Suppose someone accidentally opens his or her car door into yours while you are parked. That person immediately gets out of his car and comes over and says, "I am so sorry! I wasn't paying attention and thought your car was farther away. I would be glad to take care of the damage." More than likely, though you may feel a little frustrated, you will probably say something like, "Oh, let's forget it. I know you didn't mean to. It's okay."

It's pretty easy to extend both forgiveness and grace in this situation. And interestingly enough, we're talking here about someone you have never seen before in your life!

But when your husband or wife hurts you, isn't it interesting that giving grace and forgiveness becomes so difficult? I think this has to do with the following beliefs:

- Your perception may be that your spouse should know better and not make this kind of mistake.
- You may believe that your spouse is trying to punish you, pay you back, or get even.
- You may believe that your spouse has committed the transgression several times before and doesn't deserve grace or forgiveness.
- You may feel that your spouse just doesn't care anymore whether he or she hurts you.
- Possibly you have really never felt forgiveness or grace from others, such as your parents, someone you hurt long ago, or even God Himself. Because you have never experienced or received it, you don't know how to give it to others.

Although grace and forgiveness may be difficult to understand, receive, and extend, we must learn the process. Our marriages depend on it.

I've seen it over and over through my years of counseling. When couples really grasp the depth of the principles of grace and forgiveness, they begin to experience levels of satisfaction and happiness in their marriage beyond what they had thought possible. When couples really tap into grace and forgiveness, so many ongoing destructive issues in their marriage simply go away.

Give it a try. I encourage you to do whatever it takes to strengthen your own marriage. Your marriage is more important than whether or not your needs are being met and your own personal happiness.

Remember, happiness is a natural outcome of a healthy marriage . . . not your most important goal.

Stay committed to your marriage and make it work. Don't just "try."

Commitment is one of the major foundation stones of happy marriages. Commitment says, "I will do whatever it takes to save my marriage and make it healthy." Commitment also says, "I see myself with you when we are old and feeble, walking together, holding wrinkled hands. I see us knowing that if we part, it will be because the Lord took one of us home."

That is the kind of vision that keeps couples together, not myths about happiness.

When talking with couples who are unhappy and considering giving up, this is what I say to them: "When the door to happiness shuts, another door of opportunity opens. The problem is you are staring and grieving at the closed door so long, you can't see the new door standing wide open."

I don't know where you are right now in your thinking about your marriage, but pull up a chair. Let me ask you a couple of questions: "Have you been staring at the wrong door, perhaps a door labeled *Happiness*? Have you missed the doors God has opened to renew your marriage? Isn't it time to bring some closure to the way things used to be? Shouldn't you close some doors (like past hurts, broken promises, broken trust, embarrassing moments, and unforgiven actions or unforgiven words) permanently and pay your last respects? Don't you think it's time to let forgiveness work in your marriage?

Chapter Seven

"It's Okay to Be Rude— We're Married!"

Marriage is our last, best chance to grow up.

Joseph Barth[1]

DON'T GET ME STARTED ON THE SUBJECT OF PETS.

I love 'em. At least, the traditional ones. At this writing, I'm still not enthused about the idea of bringing home snakes, spiders, pygmy pigs, or ferrets from the pet shop.

But pets in general—you know, Fido and Fluffy—provide us human beings with something to love and to be loved by. That's all well and good, as long as we remember that . . . a pet is a pet. It's not a baby. It's not a child. In fact, it's a certified nonhuman being. As close as we may feel to these little four-footed friends, they are not one of us.

Humans are smarter. We have jobs, get married, make complex decisions, drive cars, and know how to play video games.

Animals, even the smart ones, don't do that kind of stuff. So, even though we should always treat animals humanely, we should still treat them like pets. They should get fewer rights and privileges than we do.

Some pets are extra smart. I watched a show about German shepherds who are trained to detect problems like seizures and major drops in blood sugar levels in humans. If they sense bad things are about to happen in the middle of the night, they go wake somebody up. That's pretty cool.

Animal behaviorists tell us dogs can count and learn to do things by watching humans. They say cats can solve simple problems and that adult cats have the IQ of a toddler (my toddlers were much smarter than a cat).

But the square on dogs and cats is . . . they're still part of the animal kingdom. And even if they're named Darren or Frank or Jessica, they are still German shepherds and tabbies. (In my opinion, dog psychologists and dog day spas are just a little bit over the top. Dogs shouldn't have the same luxuries we do. They are not equals no matter what culture says.)

Here's my point: I know some couples who treat their Labs and Persians better than they treat each other. Really. They have healthier feelings toward their pet than they do toward each other. I think that's pretty sad.

They seem to have bought into the marriage myth "It doesn't matter how we treat each other. After all, we're married!" They have stopped paying attention to their spouse and shifted their attention to the family pet. In fact, some of these couples seem to look to their pets for emotional needs when their marriage dives south. I know Christian couples with marital problems who have stopped sleeping in the same bed—and sleeping with the family dog instead.

Don't get me wrong. I recognize that petting the dog and connecting with the little fellow is a good thing. And nothing is better than having a dog paying you attention, especially when no one else will. I can relate completely. When my kids were young, everybody ran to the door to greet me upon arriving home from work. Now that they are all grown, the dachshund is the only one who cares enough to welcome me home. Pretty sad indeed.

I remember my dad telling a story about how his dog was one of the only things that kept him from going crazy when he was a child. His father was physically abusive, especially when he was on a drinking binge. When my dad needed to get away from the danger, he would run as fast as he could down into the field behind his house, covered high in yellow broom sage, and hunker down. Just him and his dog, Bulger.

The Bible tells us that "every good and perfect gift is from above"

(James 1:17), and our beloved pets certainly fit into the category of "good gifts from God." That being said, we shouldn't allow ourselves to reach a point in marriage where we treat our pets—or even friends or coworkers—better than we treat each other. We should remind ourselves that the Lord never addressed the relationship with our pets, friends, and neighbors as He addresses husbands and wives in Ephesians 5. He never commanded us to love our rottweiler as Jesus loved the church. He didn't command us to love and respect our poodle. But He did command each one of us to love and respect our spouse—a certified divinely created human being.

But even if our mixed-up society treats pets better than people, that doesn't mean we should.

It really does blow my mind that in the United States there seems to be more sensitivity to animals than to humans. And that some couples are sometimes more in tune with their pet's needs than with their husband's or wife's needs. I know this is true because I have counseled people like this.

FOR THE LOVE OF BERT AND ERNIE

I remember discussing this concept with a couple named Trisha and Kenny. They loved Bert and Ernie, their two Labs, more than they loved each other. I kid you not.

I remember looking at them in my counseling session and just shaking my head. "You know . . . I think you two are more in love with your dogs than you are with each other."

And they didn't deny it!

During the counseling session, they kept comparing each other to their beloved Labs: "If only Kenny would show the same devotion to me as Bert" or "At least Ernie accepts me as I am and doesn't nag me 24/7."

I sat there a little dazed by the fact that these two people had allowed their marriage "to go to the dogs." They thought more of two animals than they did each other.

It didn't take me long to draw some conclusions: "Okay, based on what you two have told me, you seem to be married to your dogs." I just kind of threw that out there and let it dangle in the air for a while. They looked at me with that "how dare you" look and shook their heads in adamant disagreement.

"Okay," I prodded. "So, you think I am off base, right?"

Kenny was the first to answer. "Well a little. That's pretty harsh to say."

Trisha added, "Yes, that's a little hard, but our Labs have never treated me like Kenny has."

Bingo.

There was a part of me that wanted to belly laugh, and part of me that wanted to cry for this sweet young couple who had so much life ahead of them and so much fantastic potential going for them.

I decided to give them the benefit of the doubt. "Okay, maybe you're right. Maybe that was a little harsh. But let me ask you a question—what do you do when one of your Labs poops on the carpet?"

Again, I get the "this guy is a psycho nut" look.

Trisha spoke up with a little attitude and said proudly, "I just clean it up!"

"Okay, Ken. What about you?"

"Pretty much the same," he said.

I stared at them like a teacher talking to a third grader who missed the teaching point and asked, "Well, what do you guys do when one of you 'messes up the carpet'? In other words, what do you do when one of you mistreats the other, shows disrespect, or makes a mistake like leaving dirty dishes in the sink?"

Silence. Wheels were spinning a hundred miles an hour in their heads. Neither was willing to answer until I repeated the question.

"Well, I, I tend to overreact," Ken said with a little embarrassment.

"What does that look like?" I urged.

"Uh, not too good. I either shout at Trisha or I get mad and stomp out of the house."

"Trisha, how do you respond to Ken's 'messes'?"

"Pretty much the same way," she confessed with a childish tone.

After a moment of silence Trisha finally added, "Boy, we have picked up some pretty bad habits as far as how we treat each other, haven't we?"

I agreed. It didn't take this couple long to realize that they really were treating the Labs better than they were treating each other.

The fact is God blessed each one of us with a spouse who has divine worth. That person is beautiful by divine design, more valuable than any costly possession on this earth, and highly valued in the eyes of the Creator. And God isn't pleased when we treat His treasure like yesterday's trash.

Being married does not give us a license to mistreat each other. The vows we made to "love, honor, cherish . . . for richer or poorer, in sickness and health . . . till death do us part" didn't just expire like a car warranty after the thirty-sixth payment.

God doesn't forget our vows. He hears them and records them in His record book. He holds us to them, no matter what excuse we come up with. Just as we will be held accountable about how we respond to the poor, the prisoner, and the outcast, we will also have to answer for our wedding vows on the day of judgment (see Matthew 25).

FIXING YOUR "WANT TO"

I've seen a number of marriages destroyed by big fights, big disagreements, and big misunderstandings.

But it's a funny thing . . . I've seen even more marriages get into trouble over a buildup of *little* things. Little habits. Little annoyances. Little discourtesies. Little cutting remarks. Little acts of thoughtlessness. Believe me, the time will come when little becomes big.

Little things can drive people crazy. Think of that door with the squeaking hinge. Think of the drip-drip-dripping faucet. Think of the neighbor's dog, barking nonstop. Think of the single hair you find on your dinner plate at a restaurant.

If you truly love your spouse and value your marriage, you really need to take little annoying habits seriously. If one spouse develops such a habit that causes significant trouble with the other, then it may be time to consider making a change—or at least a good faith attempt. Some behaviors, of course, are easier to change than others. If you are a gum popper and it drives your wife crazy, you should probably try giving up the gum. It's the minute, irritating habits that we should be willing to change if they become an issue for our spouse.

Here are some common annoying habits couples have expressed to me through the years. Maybe, just maybe, you might recognize one or two of them.

- Not emptying the wastebasket when it's full.
- Leaving wet towels on the sink.
- Picking fingernails at the dinner table.
- Leaving the toilet seat up.
- Leaving drawers and cabinet doors open.
- Putting your (shod) feet on the furniture.
- Using headaches or being too tired as an excuse for not having sex.
- Referring to your spouse using baby names such as Honey, Tootsie, and Sweetie in public.
- Arguing like children around friends.
- Criticizing your spouse in public with sarcasm or giving insults that are cloaked in humor.
- Making negative remarks about what the other is wearing.
- Nagging.
- Watching TV or typing on the computer while your spouse is trying to communicate something.
- Not stopping and asking for directions when lost.

Most of these habits are examples of things—small as they may seem—that can cause a great deal of marital pain. These habits are like a small pebble in your shoe that can rub you raw. And the frustration and anger that result from minor annoying habits can build until small problems turn into bigger ones such as: resentment, dislike, despising, and avoiding. The fact is, most of the habits I mentioned above are things that we can change.

Let me offer some suggestions on changing minor habits.

Accept the fact that you have *such a habit.* Changing an irritating habit begins with accepting the fact that what you've been doing isn't acceptable. If the action is something your spouse repeatedly reacts to negatively, that's a good indication it's something that you should change. Ask yourself, "Is my spouse's frustration really worth the payoff?" Though you may receive some level of comfort or satisfaction from the habit, it may not be worth the tension or hurt it causes in your marriage.

Realize it. Realize that though this is something *you* are comfortable with and that it doesn't bother you, it's probably not healthy to continue it if it bothers the other. I know, this all sounds very simple and elementary. But trust me, it is a fundamental principle you need to consider in order to maintain peace in relationships. It just isn't true that marriage means you're free to just "relax" and do whatever you feel like doing.

Change it. Stop talking about it and take action. It's good to say, "I am changing," but it's better to prove it. Start by making a goal to refrain from your unpleasant habit for one day. If you mess up, confess it, apologize, and try again the next day.

Check it. Check your "want to" level. Sometimes changing a bad habit is a matter of will—"Will I do it or not?" It's easy to be stubborn and obstinate. We can easily develop an attitude of revenge bythinking, *I'll show you* or *I'll teach you to nag.* Though easy to fall into, this approach usually backfires by adding more trouble to an existing problem.

When I was a teenager and failed to accomplish something, my dad reminded me that it was an attitude issue, not an ability issue. Things I said that I *couldn't* do were often things that I just didn't *want* to do. With a stern voice and eyebrows pointing to the ground, he would challenge me, "Son, you just need to get your 'want to' fixed. You can do anything you want to do."

Amazingly enough, he was right 99 percent of the time.

Couples who learn to monitor their "want to" and make the appropriate adjustments have more successful marriages than those who respond with blame, complaints, and criticisms.

EASIER SAID THAN DONE

Some habits are more difficult to quit than others.

Nelson had been a smoker since he was fifteen. Sherry knew he smoked when they married, and it didn't bother her . . . until they had their first child. Then Sherry's attitude about her husband's smoking habit changed. She expected him to stop smoking for their baby, and she also wanted him to stop for his own health so he'd be around for many years to come for their child. Because she felt passionate about this issue, she expected her husband would quit on his own.

Nelson loved both the baby and Sherry deeply and agreed with her thinking. However, agreeing with his wife didn't make it any easier for Nelson to quit a lifelong habit.

Things got worse before they got better.

Almost every day, Sherry nagged and pushed Nelson to quit.

Not surprisingly, Nelson dug in his heels and started to avoid Sherry. She began to believe that Nelson no longer cared about her or their baby. Nelson, on the other hand, thought Sherry cared more about her beliefs than about him.

Finally, after months of nagging and Nelson stonewalling, Sherry realized that her approach was not the answer. She decided to be the first to attempt to get out of the rut they had fallen into.

She humbled herself and decided to take the first step: "Nelson," she said, "I realize I was wrong for expecting you to stop smoking cold turkey. I want you to know I was wrong. I appreciate that you still care about us and only want what's best for our child and me. I love you for that. I sincerely respect you."

Almost immediately the tension lessened between the two.

Sherry showed tremendous leadership by being the first to wave the white flag. Though she backed off and apologized for her attitude and actions, she was not surrendering her beliefs. She still felt the same way about Nelson's smoking, but realizing that her passion had caused her to act inappropriately, she made healthy adjustments.

When she accepted that nagging didn't help and admitted it, this affected Nelson positively. Sherry's humility and leadership prompted Nelson to make a courageous move as well. Although he had been smoking for many years and giving it up would be difficult, Nelson felt he could at least try, for the sake of his marriage and for his baby.

He didn't stop smoking overnight. In fact, he transitioned from smoking to dipping, then to chewing gum. Sometimes Sherry felt he had swapped one bad habit for another. But although change was slow, Nelson eventually kicked the habit. Certain behaviors are difficult to change and require patience and understanding. We need to show our mate the same level of patience we expect while we try to lose weight, exercise regularly, or stop using dirty language.

We also have to accept that there may be some habits, which may never change. No one appreciates being forced into changing. It is better for the change to come from within, an internal desire versus an eternal force. Successful couples learn to accept the unchangeables in each other but continue to try to change where they can.

A LESSON FROM THE AIRLINE INDUSTRY

Rhonda and I were on our way to Nashville to visit with the financial guru Dave Ramsey and learn a little more about his ministry. When we arrived at the airport, we noticed that there seemed to be an extra long line at our airline's counter. After waiting in line for over an hour, we finally reached an attendant. I asked her a simple question and she snapped back at me. I thought, *Wow, what did I say?* I ignored her reaction and asked another question.

"Well, I don't know," she replied. "You should have found that out before you came here!"

Okay Lord, I thought, *there is one thing I really struggle with ... rude people.* So, I decided to simply call the older lady's attention to the fact she was being rude.

"Ma'am, if you haven't noticed, I have been very nice with you. However, you have been very sharp in answering every question I have raised."

She immediately cut me off, slammed her pen on the counter, and shouted, "I have had enough of people like you! Get someone else to wait on you!" She stormed off. I looked around. Every person in the airport seemed to be staring at me as if I had just shot Big Bird.

Rhonda and I looked at each other. "Can you believe that?" I said.

"No, that was wild."

About that time another angry-looking attendant walked up. "Sir, do we need to call security?"

"Look, it wasn't me. It was your attendant."

"Well, that's not what I heard."

"Okay. Please, can I speak to your manager?"

"She's busy," the other attendant snapped.

I looked down the row, and I noticed someone with a different color uniform on. I went over and asked if she might be a supervisor. "Yes, I am," she said quietly. I explained what had happened. She apologized and said she would address it.

I noticed she looked as if she were about to cry. I waited a second. Then she composed herself and said, "Sir, I am very sorry. Everyone here is angry, hurt, and scared. We just found out that our company has filed for bankruptcy and that we will all probably lose our retirement."

Oh my goodness, I thought. *No wonder these poor people are so upset.* After consoling the lady, we took our bags and headed out, thanking God that I had a job and a retirement still in place.

Just like the woman at the airline counter, your spouse may be going through something you don't know about. The next time your spouse makes a curt remark, forgets to keep a promise, or overreacts to a simple request, think about what might be influencing his or her actions. And remember that your actions or reactions can either make the situation better or worse.

Any action strategically planned by a large corporation—or by a husband named Joe—affects real people with real heartbeats. The action may seem justified, necessary, and legitimate. But we must remember that *when it comes to relationships, every action produces a reaction.* If you touch a plastic animal hanging from a mobile over the baby's crib, what happens? Touching one affects the balance and stability of the others.

TEENS AND TENSION

When we mistreat each other, when conflict reigns in our marriage, it affects others. This is especially true if you have children. To illustrate, let me share with you a model I've been working on—much of it based on my own personal observation and experience in working with families through the years.

The basic idea is that marriage tension in the home can lead children—and especially teens—to avoid natural interaction with one or both parents. It usually boils down to a diminished relationship with the dad, in particular.

Long-term tension eventually leads children to avoid and eventually to disengage from their parents or family—emotionally, physically, or both. Disengagement typically leads to withdrawal. Withdrawal sets the stage for the child, especially teens, to seek engagement outside the home through such avenues as gangs, drugs, pornography, harmful websites and chat rooms. These activities seem to medicate the pain that the child is feeling—but they also exacerbate the tension between parent and child. The added tension layers onto the already present tension in the couple's marriage. Escalation occurs and the cycle repeats over and over.

It's not a pretty picture.

One obvious point of intervention for couples as well as marriage leaders should be to address the unhealthy, ongoing tension in the marriage. The idea is to stop the source—to defuse the energy—of the continual cycle. If parents change attitudes and behaviors that are causing tension, the negative reaction of the child acting out and the additional tension between the couple and the child can be positively reduced or possibly eliminated.

When a marriage goes bad, it has a profound effect on the entire family. *Marriage isn't just about the couple.* Don't let anyone scam you on this. A healthy marriage should be the strongest foundation for building and maintaining health throughout the family. Therapists, youth pastors, and social workers have known for years that a teen's attitude, emotional health, and behavior is often a barometer of what's going on in the marriage of that particular home.

God expects us to honor our spouses. He even tells husbands that he won't listen to their prayers if they are mistreating their wives. He takes this very seriously—and so should we.

Chapter Eight

"I Shouldn't Have to Ask"

"By the time a man can read a
woman like a book, he needs bifocals."

—Bob Phillips (author and counselor)[1]

FROM THE TIME OUR YOUNGEST, Ben, was able to talk, he was (and still is) predominantly a concrete thinker. Don't bother talking to him in abstract terms—he prefers things spelled out in black-and-white.

When he was four years old, he couldn't wrap his mind around the concept of time like other kids his age. It wasn't a matter of intelligence; his test scores rocketed off the charts. It was all about how he was wired to learn and grasp concepts.

If we told Ben that he was going to school "tomorrow," he wouldn't get that. But if we told him that "when the sun goes down and it becomes dark and then the sun comes up again, you will go to school," he got that. If we told him that "when *Power Rangers* comes on and goes off, then it will be time to get dressed for the party," he got that as well.

When he was in the fourth grade, his teacher called us and asked for a meeting. She said that he had shut down, tuned out, and didn't seem to care about his work.

Well, we met with the teacher and found out that as concrete as Ben was, his teacher was about as general—the opposite extreme. She thought she was communicating clearly, her nonspecific approach was sailing right over Ben's little head.

Ben always wanted specifics. Once he got them, he usually obeyed without protest.

After seeing the core problem, the counselor side of me kicked in and I made a suggestion. I offered to draft and print thirty copies (thirty days worth) of "communication" sheets. Before the last bell rang each day, Ben would fill in what he understood the assignment to be, the teacher would sign it if it was what she intended, and Ben would bring it home. We would check the sheet each evening, and if Ben was still confused, we would send the note back to the teacher asking for more specific information and asking her to be concrete in her instructions.

This worked wonders for Ben. His grades went from Ds to As overnight. Also, the accountability of having to show what he was assigned and then having our help to make sure he did the assignment was good discipline for him.

The teacher was a generalist; Ben was a true concrete thinker. If we had not understood Ben's learning style and accepted that God made him this way, it could have been devastating for years to come. We could have compared Ben to the rest of the kids in his class and constantly berated him for not being up to par. But no child responds well to that kind of motivation. Neither do our spouses.

"BUT I SHOULDN'T HAVE TO TELL THEM!"

Many spouses are like Ben and his teacher—they don't understand each other. Or they buy into certain myths such as "I shouldn't have to tell my spouse what I want. He should just know . . . she should just understand."

Some make the common mistake of comparing their spouse to others. If you ever start to fall into that trap, the red warning lights should start to flash before the words roll off your tongue. Comparison only creates hurt, resentment, pain, and distance. It does nothing for a marriage.

Speaking in a much different context, the apostle Paul noted the habit of some of the false teachers of his day when he said, "When they measure themselves by themselves and compare themselves with themselves, they are not wise" (2 Corinthians 10:12).

Not wise!

And that applies to comparisons within a marriage too. Understanding within a marriage is a precious, sometimes fragile commodity, and will not be helped by dragging irrelevant comparisons into the discussion.

Sometimes as spouses we have to go to great lengths to understand, explain, and creatively tackle a given problem or dilemma in our relationship. We shouldn't get hung up on asking for what we need, sometimes more than once.

If you ask your doctor to help you deal with a health concern, but he forgets to bring it up by the time you leave your appointment, what do you do? You ask again. Or in a worst-case scenario, you remind your doctor on the next visit. You don't get angry and overreact, and you don't hold it against your doctor. You accept the fact that he or she has 289 other patients, is struggling with malpractice insurance, and has a truckload of issues to consider each day.

We should have the same attitude in marriage.

Let me say this slowly: If we need something, we *usually* have to ask for it. If we still don't get a response, sometimes we have to ask again or ask in a different way.

Most of the time your husband or wife is not a vicious person who willfully withholds what you need, laughing wickedly up his or her sleeve. Often it's a matter of not listening, not understanding, or maybe it's just plain old forgetfulness.

"But I shouldn't have to ask for something as important as this," some insist.

Want my professional response? "Why not?"

This is one of those long-held pieces of counterfeit wisdom that seems stealthily to have slipped into our belief systems. And it's as phony as a yellow three-dollar bill. Where does this myth come from? My suspicion is that Satan is the culprit. He may not be able to tempt you into an affair or embezzle thousands of dollars from work, but if he can get you to buy into a myth that causes constant division and sinful disarray in your marriage, he's got you just the same. Evil prefers no one method. Whatever works will do.

How serious is this? It's life-and-death serious.

Some couples divorce over this myth, shattering families, creating negative impact for generations. The frustration, hurt, and resentment build up until people see no way out.

We can't read each other's mind. Believe me, I have tried. My wife has tried. She can't do it, either.

I have heard hundreds of wives portray their pitiful lot in life because they "have to ask" their husbands for something because he doesn't think of it first: "He just doesn't care for me if I have to keep reminding him. It's a sign of disrespect and indifference."

No it's not. More likely, it's a sign of being human.

Likewise, I have heard droves of Christian husbands drone on like a hungry child who was sent to bed without dinner because they had to ask their wives for sex: "But she knows I need sex. God made me this way. I can't help it. She should know this by now."

Hey guys, listen, we all agree that we need sex and that our wives should read our needs like the button that pops up on the Thanksgiving turkey. But they are not always as in tune with our needs as we are.

The same is true with men reading women's faces. I remember reading a study once that revealed that men have a difficult time reading sadness on women's faces. A majority of the men in the study could easily read happiness, but a majority could not always read sadness.

"Why didn't he say something when he saw that I was sad?" I have been asked multiple times in counseling.

"Well, maybe he didn't see it."

It's hard for women to understand that. They can read a glum face on somebody clear across the mall. "Oh, look, honey, she's really sad."

Women can even talk to each other without saying a word. Just watch two women sitting by each other at church. They look at each other, one shakes her head, the other smiles, and they nod back and forth. The husbands sit there thinking, *These women have a nervous disorder.*

We are created differently, are we not?

JUST ASK FOR IT

Just because you have a need doesn't mean your spouse automatically knows. It may be so clear in your mind that you taste it, but that doesn't mean your partner has a clue about what's going on in your heart.

Are you ready for a shocker? Some women *never* reach a point in marriage where they automatically know when their husband needs sex. Since women aren't wired like we are, you may have to ask for it.

And guess what, guys? It isn't the end of the world. The world will keep turning if we don't have sex at the end of each day. (Sometimes it does feel like it though.) Ladies, don't make the mistake of thinking if you're not in the mood, then he's not either. Men pretty much keep their motors running most of the time. That could be one of the reasons the Scripture says to not withhold yourself from the other except for a limited time.

The same applies to women when they need affection. You may have told your husband what you need, but like a concrete-thinking child, he may need you to spell it out for him. Stress, frustration, or just being really tired can all be causes for us to forget things we usually remember. If you spell it over and over again, and he still doesn't respond, that moves the issue into a deeper problem—indifference. Indifference and withdrawal can be two destinations that are difficult to pull back from because you have slipped into a "I don't care anymore" mind-set.

This is absolutely applicable to both genders.

We all have wants; often they are very selfish wants. Even children learn this at an early age. "I want that" becomes a two-year-old's favorite phrase, especially while in the toy department at a store. A child has to learn that he or she can't always get everything. Some accept this better than others.

When our two older kids were little, they would come up with lists at Christmastime. Sometimes the lists would be short, maybe a page or two. When Ben was four, he thought through this request issue and came up with something that covered all the bases.

After devotions one day we asked our kids what they wanted for Christmas. The two oldest detailed their wish list quickly. Then it was Ben's turn.

"Ben, what would you like for Christmas?"

He stood up and said, "Oh, I've thought this thing through and decided I would just like a credit card!" At age four! With a credit card, he reasoned, he could cut through this list foolishness and get whatever he wanted.

Once we understand that we are all pretty selfish, "me-oriented" people by nature, we must try to get our arms around basic principles about needs and asking for them.

Here are few things I have learned about asking from my own marriage and other couples I have worked with.

1. *Pray about it before asking.* No request is too small or too big to pray about first. Talking to God about something before you talk to your spouse can make a world of difference.

2. *Give your spouse a way out.* Don't let your request become a demand. If your husband tries to meet your request and fails, let him know in advance that you will not berate, belittle, or "sigh" him into shame.

   Assure your wife (and mean it) that if it doesn't work out the way you want it, you will appreciate the fact that she tried. Be willing to talk afterward about an alternative that your wife might come up with that will still meet your needs.

3. *Suggest, don't demand.* This is especially helpful if you're one of those people who seem to come across too strong, even when that's not your intention. Maybe begin by saying, "I was wondering . . ." rather than "Okay, Buddy, this is what I need. Hand it over and nobody will get hurt."

Be tentative rather than specific: "I was thinking today about how this might work. What do you think?" Then, listen.

Remember that *you* have been thinking about this issue for possibly a long time. It may be brand-new to your spouse. Give him or her an opportunity to think about your request, and don't become resentful if he or she needs a little processing time.

If your spouse says he or she needs time to think about a new idea, it's probably true. Remember, everyone is not wired the same way. Some people have mental processes that work as fast as the latest computer chip. Others take longer to process things . . . and the disk drive grinds along for a while before a rational answer emerges. Slow down your requirement for obtaining a speedy yes or no.

4. *Don't push for a decision.* If after a reasonable amount of time, your spouse hasn't responded to your request, remind him or her, but don't pistol-whip your partner for forgetting.

5. *Be willing to take something less than what you asked for.* All good negotiators know this principle. If you can't get exactly what you are asking for, maybe having something is better than nothing. A win here may lead to a bigger win later. Also be willing to accept a no in response to your request. If you overreact, it will decrease the chances that your spouse will be open to readdressing the issue later.

ASKING IS GOOD!

What if you are on the other side of the coin? What if you're the one receiving a request?

1. *Reframe the request in your mind.* Rather than being irritated, be thankful that your spouse wants to make a request of you. A request is an indication that your spouse still cares about your marriage. The worst type of spouse is one who simply no longer cares. I would much rather work with a couple who are at odds because they haven't figured out how to communicate needs, versus a couple who are withdrawn and just don't care anymore.

2. *Don't overreact.* Breathe. Think. Process. Ponder. This is not the time to emote all over the place. Don't overreact to a request that comes across as a criticism. Think about it. Pray about it. Ask for time to mull it over and set a time to talk about it later.

3. *Don't become defensive.* Your spouse has as much right to ask for something as you do, even if it involves a change from you.

Asking is good. Even God wants us to ask for things. And He listens. Read the requests of David and Job. God listened and even allowed these men to vent a little. In the book of James, the Holy Spirit tells us, "You do not have because you do not ask" (James 4:2).

Let God teach you through your mate's request. He can certainly do that, even if the request is tinged with a little selfishness. When your spouse makes a request of you, it can show you something about yourself as well as the one making the request. You may not know your mate feels this way or is really hurting about something until he or she makes a request of you.

Good can come even from what we first perceive to be bad.

4. *Remember that part of love is enduring the stuff you don't feel you should have to put up with.* God commands us to put the other's needs above our own, to prefer the other above ourselves. Remember that love doesn't keep record of wrongs— even requests from a spouse that we feel are not warranted (1 Corinthians 13:5).

5. *Ask questions:* Be willing to say to your spouse, "Let me make sure I understand what you are saying . . ." Then repeat back what you thought your mate was asking for. Or be willing to ask him or her simply to repeat the question. When you ask your spouse to repeat something, he or she may realize it didn't come out as intended the first time and may welcome the chance to rephrase the request. Also, when you ask your partner to repeat what he or she said, you give yourself a little time to think before you respond.

"THE MORE YOU PUSH, THE MORE I RESIST"

Teresa was very structured and linear in her thinking. Her husband, Kenneth, was anything but. She could see patterns in everything; he couldn't see a pattern if his nose was embedded in one. Both were extremely intelligent people with graduate degrees, but they were wired differently and went about solving problems differently as well.

When Teresa went about solving a problem like fixing a leaky faucet, she first thought about it, researched it on the Internet, and then put her plan down on paper. She solved the problem step-by-step—A, B, C.

Teresa felt that her way was the most efficient. She liked to solve any problem that came up in a timely manner. If something was broken, it should be fixed, today or by the latest tomorrow, first thing in the morning. She didn't want to wait around. Teresa saw the drip as a river that needed to be addressed *now*, not tomorrow. It was a moral issue with her.

Kenneth was just the opposite. He liked to solve problems the way he had since he was a child, the most practical way imaginable, which often meant trying different ways until one of them worked. He saw no reason to solve problems immediately. He usually solved problems when they got big enough to interfere with his daily routine, or when the problem made someone else mad . . . like Teresa, for example.

What Teresa saw as a major leak, Kenneth saw as a drip. In his mind, he would fix the faucet when it began to pour like a stream. There were other things on his agenda that seemed to him just as, or even more, important than a leaky faucet.

Teresa and Kenneth viewed almost everything in their marriage through these two distinct sets of lenses.

Teresa saw Kenneth's approach to problems like fixing the dripping faucet, cleaning the garage, putting away his clothes, and so forth as being irresponsible. She resented that Kenneth couldn't be "thoughtful enough" or "concerned enough" to do things that she felt he should do without being asked. She viewed asking Kenneth to do these things as a way of enabling his bad habits. She yearned for the day when he would start doing things on his own (the way she wanted him to do).

Kenneth saw Teresa's approach to such situations as uptight, anal, and smothering She came across to Kenneth as a mother, not a partner.

During a counseling session one day, I asked a simple question: "What happens when you ask Kenneth to fix the faucet?"

Teresa thought a second and said, "He fixes it. Not always when I want him to, but he gets it done, usually after experimenting and making it worse before it gets better."

"And what do you do in the meantime?"

"Well, I typically complain and tell him the best way to get it done."

"And how does that help?"

"It doesn't, but I feel somebody has to say something."

"Kenneth, how does that make you feel?"

"Like a moron," he said.

"And what happens the next time Teresa asks you to do something?"

"I put it off as long as I can."

"Why?" I asked.

"Because I know that no matter what I do it will not be Teresa's way, and she will disapprove."

"Teresa, do you remember what your answer was to my question a minute ago about what happens when you ask Kenneth to fix the faucet?"

"Yes."

"You said that he fixes it, right?"

"Yes."

"Then what's the problem?"

"The problem is that I shouldn't have to *ask* him to fix the faucet."

"Yes, but you just said that he does solve the problem. He does get the job done. But the real problem seems to be that you have to ask him several times to fix the sink, just as you might ask a kid to clean up his room. Basically, Kenneth doesn't address problems the way you would prefer or in the time frame you want. Right?"

"Well, I guess that's right, but I shouldn't have to ask Kenneth . . . should I? He should care enough and respect me enough to do it without asking."

"Ummm," I said.

I had just put my finger on the problem. Teresa's expectations for Kenneth were very high, based on a simple misunderstanding about personality differences. In response to his wife's expectations, Kenneth had adopted the "old mule" attitude: "the more you push, the more I will resist." It wasn't a matter of caring or respect to Kenneth; he just saw problems differently from Teresa.

Kenneth and Teresa wanted the same things, but they both had to make some changes in order for a resolution to come about. Teresa had to accept that Kenneth would get things done, just not the way she preferred. Just because she had to ask Kenneth to do something didn't mean he was immature or that he didn't respect her. Kenneth had to learn to see Teresa's perspective on things and be sensitive to her timing sensitivity.

Teresa agreed that she would start asking Kenneth in a different way to do things she felt were important, and not overwhelm him by asking him to do everything at once in her time frame. At the beginning of the week, she wrote a list of one or two things that she wanted Kenneth to accomplish before Sunday evening. Teresa agreed to be "hands-off" at that point. She would not instruct, suggest, or remind. Kenneth agreed to get everything on the list done by Sunday evening.

It was amazing. Not only did Kenneth get the tasks done, but he often did them before his Sunday evening deadline. At times he would ask Teresa for advice on how to get things done. In fact, he stopped seeing her advice as threatening and often welcomed it. Teresa saw that there was more than one way to get things done. She began to understand that her time schedule and sense of urgency were not the same as Kenneth's and not always the only way. She also stopped being offended when Kenneth didn't see things the way she did. She learned to simply ask him and then remind him if he forgot her request.

HOW TO REALLY LISTEN

One of the most basic things that any couple can do to strengthen their marriage is learn how to be better listeners. Effective communication involves both talking and listening.

Do you want to improve your listening skills? Let me give you some basic, practical suggestions.

- *Learn to really listen, not just hear.* You say you hear your spouses, employers, friends, and even those you want to help, but are you really listening?

  I was taught in Communication 101 that most people only comprehend and retain about one-fourth of what they hear. If true, this means that many responses, reactions, and feelings go misunderstood, especially between spouses.

  When you listen effectively to your spouse, you demonstrate deep respect and care for him or her. When you really listen, you communicate that what your spouse is feeling and thinking is really important to you. You are sending the message, "I care about what you're feeling, thinking, or going through."

- *Give your full attention.* Put aside all distractions. Unplug the iPod from your ears. Turn the ringer off on your phone. If you're at home, turn off the TV, computer, or music. If you're in the car, turn off the radio. Put your cell phone on vibrate. As much as possible, create an environment that will not allow your attention and focus to shift from the person to whom you are listening. Send the signal to your spouse that you really are more interested in what he or she has to say than anything else that may be going on around you.

- *Don't make judgments or draw conclusions before your spouse finishes speaking.* Don't respond until your spouse has completed her entire thought or sentence. Try to remain objective about what is being said. Control any temptation to be offended or draw conclusions before you hear the complete story. Stop thinking of ways to solve your spouse's problem or ways to launch a counterattack until after you have heard everything.

  The Bible teaches us that we should "be quick to listen, slow to speak" (James 1:19). If we could just master this one biblical truth in our relationships, just think how our marriages would improve!

- *Listen with your body. Maintain a natural and comfortable measure of eye contact with your spouse as he or she is speaking.* Lean toward your spouse as he or she speaks. Let your facial expressions communicate interest and concern. Don't cross your arms or sit with your legs sprawled. Don't slouch in your chair. Don't shake your legs, pat your foot, or tap your fingernails on the desk. Stay away from any action that may be distracting to the one speaking. Make sure you're not communicating with your body "I really don't want to hear what you have to say."

I have witnessed conflicted couples turn their marriage around in a short period of time simply by learning and putting into practice these basic listening skills. Learning to really listen to your spouse is definitely one of the best things you can do for your marriage.

Chapter Nine

"Conflict Is Bad"

Like lightning and thunder, conflict
can be loud, scary, and unnerving.
But like a good thunderstorm, healthy
conflict can also help clear the air.

I HATED CONFLICT GROWING UP. I hated fighting. My brother, on the other hand, seemed energized by a good brawl. He would pick a fight with me just because he was bored. He was one of the bravest people I knew. He would stand his ground with boys twice his size. He didn't back down from anyone.

When we were eighteen and nineteen, we made the fatal mistake of dating sisters. That tore us apart. Like the Civil War, it came down to brother against brother. After my brother accused me of "talking about his girlfriend," he came into my room and started poking me in the chest. I hated fighting, but when someone poked me in the chest—and there was a girl issue involved in the mix—it was too much for me. Before I knew it, before he knew it, I had clobbered him right in the mouth. The punch literally put him against the wall.

I can still close my eyes and see a "what was that" look on his face.

It stunned me too. I didn't realize doing those pushups every night and working for a brick mason that summer could work those kinds of wonders.

As my brother began to come around, he started trying to get up. He was pretty shaken, but I knew that as soon as he could get vertical, he would come after me. I wasn't wrong. Though my anger had died down, his was just starting. I regretted that I had lost control because the ending was worse than the beginning.

When Rhonda and I married, I discovered that she was a conflict-avoider, like me. The difference was that if you pushed me far enough or I hurt enough, I would go from avoiding conflict to pushing it. But Rhonda hated conflict with everything in her. She had watched family and friends struggle with conflict for years and was determined that she would not follow the same pattern.

But in time I realized that as much as both of us disliked conflict, we had to go through it to reach the other side. I just didn't know the correct way to go about it. I would immediately jump into the argument with accusations and start passing out judgments. Rhonda would try to walk away. I would pursue her. It turned disastrous every time.

Like everyone, I stumble with this myself from time to time. But I've also learned some principles that have helped me grow in my ability to manage sharp disagreements.

The key to effective conflict is learning how to *engage* and when to put it *on hold*. Engaging in conflict may be necessary at times, but it's also important to know how to begin and when to walk away.

Conflict isn't what kills marriages. Conflict isn't always bad. It is conflict gone wild that kills marriages.

RELATIONAL ARSON

You can't live in Colorado without learning about wildfires. This place can become so tinder dry that it can light up in the blink of an eye. In most places, Coloradans are not allowed to burn trash, and in certain neighborhoods you can't even have a barbecue with an open flame.

It takes some getting used to.

In the South, where I come from, we burn everything. If you don't like something, you take it out in the backyard and set fire to it.

In Florida, it didn't matter how much stuff you burned. The ground was so wet that there was no danger of forest fires. Here in Colorado, it's a very different story.

A couple I counseled not too long ago illustrates how bad conflict can happen to good marriages. She was a research assistant and IT consultant; he was a wildfire specialist and fought forest fires. Ironically, the main problem in their marriage was that they were starting fires (arguments) and allowing them to burn out of control.

Chrissy would bring up a topic because Tim never would. By the time she got the courage to bring something up, she was flaming mad herself. The fire immediately jumped from her to Tim. At that point he felt attacked. She felt attacked. He felt hurt because she was so harsh. She felt betrayed because he wouldn't talk about anything until she got upset. Negative patterns like these continued to smolder in their marriage for years. The couple seemed to have most other things in their marriage under control, except this one area.

The sad reality is that you can do all the other stuff perfectly in marriage, but if you can't control the way you handle conflict, it will ultimately undo and destroy all the good things in your marriage, including intimacy, mutual respect, attitudes, and commitment.

After a few minutes into our first session, I recognized their problem.

Chrissy and Tim's main problem was ruts—unhealthy patterns of conflict. They started each conversation negatively with stinging words and judgmental tones. After the negative startups, things just escalated. Instead of stopping and starting over, they let the dysfunction roll downhill like a snowball. Before the conflict ended, they were yelling down each other's throats. They seemed always to be just about to cross the line between arguing and physical contact. Tim said he knew that they were dancing on the edge, and he wanted to get help before the situation got out of control.

To help Tim and Chrissy understand better what was happening, I asked Tim about wildfires. (I knew that Chrissy did some research work for the National Forest Service and that she understood the principles of wildfires almost as well as Tim.)

Tim explained, "In order for a wildfire to start, there have to be three things: something to burn (fuel), air (oxygen), and a source of heat to bring the fuel to its flash point. If your fuel (wood, sticks, grass) is stressed by being too dry, or is small and loosely arranged on the ground, you've got trouble. It will light up really fast. Then the fire will escalate out of control quickly."

"Well," I replied, "how do you use that knowledge to fight a fire?"

Tim went on eagerly. This was comfortable ground, something he knew about—and much easier to talk about than his contentious marriage.

"The key is to take away any one of those three things. Then you can get the fire under control and eventually put it out. But if those three components continue to be in the picture (fuel, air, and heat), the fire will keep burning."

"Interesting," I said.

You must understand that though Tim's fire lecture was engaging, I wasn't just sitting back and enjoying the show. I knew where I wanted to go with this and Tim's story was helping me get there.

"Okay," I said, "tell me about wind. How does wind play into the picture here?"

"Oh!" Tim said with vigor. "That is a big one. When you add outside influences, something in addition to the three factors—like wind—the fire will just get worse and even do unnatural things like move faster up a hill versus down the hill." Tim wound down his story at this point and seemed a little suspicious. I guess he caught onto the fact that I was taking him somewhere, and he wasn't sure if he liked the direction.

I let silence linger in the room for a few seconds. Tim and Chrissy waited patiently as they watched me gather my thoughts. I moved my chair close to them, took them both by the hands and looked into their eyes, and said softly but firmly: "Tim and Chrissy, let me cut to the chase. In your careers you guys fight fires, but in your marriage you start them and fan them until they are out of control.

"You guys are what I call relational arsonists. You are like many couples who have allowed patterns and conditions to become so incredibly ripe that fires break out almost every time the two of you try to communicate. Then once the fire rages, you both keep doing things that make it run uphill. You fight so much that the fuel is ready for the flame. At this point in your marriage, a conversation only needs a small spark to set you guys off. Previous fires, ongoing hurts, and daily stress have pulled the intimacy out of your relationship. Your marriage is as dry as it can be, and you don't seem to know what to do about it. Instead of learning new ways to deal with conflict, you just seem to keep starting fires and fanning them. No wonder your marriage is crumbling. Your actions, combined with holding on to previous hurts from the last flare-up, just continue to make your fires hotter than before."

I shifted gears a little at this point. "Conflict is very much like fire. It can be good. Fire cooks our food. An ignition and spark move our cars. It keeps us from freezing to death in winter, and it lights up the night so we can see. It directs us. But I don't have to tell either of you that fire out of control can destroy, kill, and change lives forever. Uncontrolled conflict can do the same. It can destroy any marriage in a short period of time."

I continued, "The way you two are handling conflict is similar to drying your backyard out with a huge heater, then throwing dry pine needles in it, pouring on a little gas here and there, dropping a match, and then standing back and wondering, *How did this all happen?* You both are not only responsible for starting fires in your marriage, you keep them going by adding more fuel. As you watch the fire get out of control, you blame each other for being the arsonist.

"Tim . . . Chrissy . . . here's the bottom line, based on what you have told me. If you keep doing the things you are doing regarding how you handle conflict, nothing will be left but ashes in your marriage. Only memories, bitter memories. You can't keep doing the same things, following the same unhealthy pattern and expect different results."

I opened my Bible to James 3:6, and read it out loud. "The tongue also is a fire, a world of evil among the parts of the body. It corrupts the whole person, sets the whole course of his life on fire, and is itself set on fire by hell."

I continued by saying, "And, let me tell you something else, the fire you guys start not only affects you, but it affects your job performance, your physical and mental health, your extended family, and your church family. I can predict that your kids are choking from the smoke as well. Not only are your actions hurting the marriage God blessed you with, but you are teaching your children to follow in your footsteps. Is that what you really want?"

I felt kind of guilty because I had shot so straight with them. I took off my preacher's hat and laid it to the side and waited, just like any good counselor will do when he knows his client's heart has been touched. At moments like these, silence can work in powerful ways.

These two beautiful, loving, good-hearted people sat stricken—stricken with the truth. They began to wipe tears from their eyes, holding their heads down. Inwardly, I thanked God for giving me that analogy of the wildfire. I knew that they got it, and recognized that the patterns that had developed in their marriage were simply wrong. They wanted something better for their two toddlers back at home. They just needed to find a better path.

In the weeks to come, I worked with Tim and Chrissy on the right ways to handle fire in their marriage. They responded well. They began to shift from being relational arsonists to capable firefighters. They learned to stop the habits, change the patterns, get out of the ruts of the past, and form new ones.

The clouds of stress and tension that hovered over their marriage every day ultimately went away. Moisture, intimacy, came back. Joy returned. Their home became a refuge once again.

THE FOUR HORSEMEN

Dr. John Gottman did a study on marital conflict and found that there were four general destructive patterns couples fall into. He called these patterns "The Four Horsemen." He used the analogy of the four horsemen in the book of Revelation, a graphic image representing destruction and complete devastation.

Dr. Gottman conducted this study over a sixteen-year period. He actually observed couples in a "love lab" and watched how they interacted. He had them hooked up to sensors that measured blood pressure and heart rate, took blood samples during arguments to measure testosterone, adrenaline, and so on. From this study with over seven hundred couples, he identified four general patterns of destructive conflict: criticism, contempt, defensiveness, and stonewalling. He concluded from his research that if these patterns continued, the chances of divorce were very high.[1]

So, let's take a look at these "four horsemen" that can so easily destroy a marriage.

1. Criticism

By Dr. Gottman's definition, criticism is different from a legitimate complaint. A complaint is when you legitimately voice a concern to your spouse with the right approach. Criticism goes further. This is when you and your spouse begin to attack each other's character and make accusations and inflammatory judgments. Let's imagine Chrissy said the following: "Tim, you are so stupid. I have asked you a thousand times not to leave the garage door up. Didn't your crazy mom teach you anything?" Words like these are more than just a complaint. Chrissy has upped the ante by attacking Tim's character, as well as his mom's character.

If Chrissy had complained instead of criticized, she might have said something like this: "Tim, would you mind shutting the garage door? When you leave it open, the cat runs out and I have to stop cooking dinner to find her." That's a legitimate complaint.

2. Contempt

This is conveying utter disgust for the other person. This can be done by using a certain tone of voice, rolling your eyes, sighing loudly, talking under your breath, or using contemptuous body language such as crossing your arms, distasteful gestures, or turning your back while the other is talking. You can also convey contempt by using malicious, cutting statements, which can be easily cloaked in "humor." The sad thing is that this type of humor is only used to hurt and embarrass your spouse, sometimes in public. Just because it's humorous doesn't mean it's okay.

3. Defensiveness

This is pretty self-explanatory. It means being hypersensitive to any form of complaint or even healthy instruction. Defensiveness displays an "it's you, not me" type of attitude or behavior. When you become defensive, you not only fight your spouse, but you fight yourself. This really only escalates the original problem.

4. Stonewalling

This behavior typically follows on the heels of the other horses. Often couples trot down the roads of criticism, contempt, and defensiveness, until one or both resorts to the next stage—stonewalling. This is when you or your spouse simply tunes out or becomes like a stone wall.

We men are pros at this. We reach a point where we're so tired of trying to stop the conflict that we simply give up. We stonewall in an attempt to prevent ourselves from becoming "flooded" or physiologically overwhelmed.

The truth is no one likes to try to talk to a wall. But that is what you become when you close up, turn your back, and tune out your spouse. Stonewalling sends the signal that you don't care anymore, that you are walking out and leaving the other one to put out the fires. You have decided to just let the fires burn.

Don't let any of these four horsemen enter your marriage. Once they've invaded, stomping all over your hopes and dreams, they're tough to get rid of.

THE BLAME GAME

Since marriage is made up of two people, occasionally blaming each other for personal mistakes seems almost inevitable. Serious problems, however, can develop when blaming takes up residence and becomes a way of life.

Blaming is the easiest thing in the world.

It's oh-so-easy to transfer the fault for decisions, actions, thoughts, and words to the other partner instead of owning up to the mistake. In fact, the practice of blaming started with Adam pointing the accusing finger at Eve for enticing him to eat the forbidden fruit. (Eve turned right around and blamed the serpent.) And it's been going on ever since. Some couples have come to believe that it is less problematic to transfer the responsibility of uncontrolled temper or other individual blunders to their partner than to accept responsibility by saying, "You know, I was wrong. It wasn't your fault at all; it was mine."

If blaming occurs during an argument, it will likely only cause additional pain and scarring. You are likely adding fuel to the fire. The unjust practice of marital blaming shifts the focus and responsibility to your spouse. And how does that make your mate feel? Like you've turned on him. Like you've landed a punch when she wasn't on guard. Your partner feels hurt and will either retaliate with additional fervor or simply retreat into isolation. The normal response pattern to blaming is anger, retaliation, withdrawal, isolation, and resentment. And the sad thing is, the problem remains unresolved. Now you not only have to deal with the original issue, you also have to deal with the fact that you unfairly shifted the burden of responsibility to your spouse.

The more you shift the blame and refuse to accept responsibility and make necessary changes in your own life, the more damaged and isolated you and your spouse may become. No one appreciates being made a "scapegoat." Who wants to be cordial and intimate with someone who treats you that way?

Once you get into the blaming habit, it snowballs and naturally places you on a course to blame everyone in your life, including your mother and father for giving you life in the first place. Or maybe even God, for allowing the circumstances in which you find yourself.

The truth is, we are responsible for our own feelings, emotions, and actions and have little control over what other people do.

As the old saying goes, "You can kick the garbage can but you'll have to pick up the trash." You can choose to blame your spouse for what occurs in your marriage, but you will suffer the consequences. It is much healthier to accept and correct your own mistakes first than to attempt to correct those of your spouse.

FIGHTING THE GOOD FIGHT

Suppose you pulled up to your house after work one day, and as you looked up at your home, you saw smoke billowing out of the windows on the top floor. What if you called your wife on your cell phone and the conversation went something like this: "Hi, Honey. I'm in the driveway. How was your day? Oh, mine was pretty good too. Hey, did you call the cable company? Good. I hope they finally get that problem cleared up. Oh, by the way, have you noticed that smoke is coming out of the windows upstairs?"

You would never have a conversation like this, right? And you would consider someone who did to be an idiot. And you would be right.

But haven't we all been guilty of conversations like this when it comes to conflict gone wild in our marriage? Smoke may be pouring out of our marriage, warning us of danger, and we just keep moving on with life, avoiding the issue, assuming the problem will eventually fix itself.

But could there actually be a potential for something positive to grow out of your conflict?

Think of a lightning storm on a warm summer night. Although a thunderstorm is often terrifying and loud, after the storm the air feels cleansed, possibly due to the production of molecules that help clean the air of dust. The same is true when we experience and deal with conflict in marriage in an appropriate way. Even if it is loud, scary, and perhaps animated, conflict can help to clear our relationships of contaminates and move us in a positive direction.

Here are a few things to remember in reframing the way you see and deal with conflict.

• *Start the right way.* If you start a disagreement with loud words, harsh statements, and judgmental accusations, you have started badly.

These are negative approaches.

Like a computer, if you put the wrong things in, wrong things will appear on the screen. If you start a conversation harshly with anger and "venom," that is what the outcome will look like. You can't attack, threaten, and chew people out—even those you love—if you expect them to respond in the right way. The Bible teaches us to be kind to each other, tenderhearted, not cruel, mean, and rude. Husbands, if you treat your wife rudely, do you expect her to roll over and play dead? Wives, when you push your husband to the edge of anger by railing and nagging, do you expect him to respond in kindness? What if you took that approach with your coworkers on a daily basis? You wouldn't last too long. Someone would quit, or both of you would get fired.

Don't start an argument with "You never . . . " or "You always . . . " or "Here you go again." Accusations only add oxygen and wind to the flame. Start an argument the right way if you want to keep the fire from blazing out of control.

• *Don't try to ignore the conflict.* I have learned that denying a problem, sweeping it under the proverbial rug, doesn't make it better. If you deny you have cancer after the doctor says you do, your denial doesn't make you better.

• *Don't fight dead issues.* Don't make something a mountain when it's only a speed bump. Sometimes minor irritations are better left alone. Choose your battles. Ask yourself, "Is this really worth bringing up again? Should I leave it alone instead of bringing it back to life?" Use common sense. Or at least talk to someone who has some. Remember that one of the characteristics of true love is that it "keeps no record of wrongs" (1 Corinthians 13:5).

• *Get your timing right.* Don't try to resolve conflict at the wrong time or place. If you're going to discuss something important, try to create an environment where you can be calm and not disturbed. Use a little discipline and wait until the kids are in bed. Turn off the TV. Take the phone off the hook. Unplug the computer so you don't hear e-mails pinging into your mailbox. Don't try to solve problems during times of great stress or grief. Again use common sense and practical discernment.

By the way, don't try to solve serious issues over the phone or via e-mail. Neither of these forms of communication allows you to see each other's body language and heart. You can only see your spouse's heart when you are looking into his or her eyes.

• *Listen intentionally.* We married people ought to stencil the words of James 1:19 on the inside of our eyelids: "Everyone should be quick to listen, slow to speak and slow to become angry." Learn to listen with your whole attention, rather than having half your mind occupied with preparing your statement of defense.

Make a commitment that you will control your tongue by not saying what you are thinking for the next few minutes. Let the other finish speaking. Don't interrupt. As I said, choose your battles. Assess whether what you are about to say is really worth risking the "fallout that might result." If it isn't kind, don't say it.

Wives, allow your husband time to think. If he needs time to process what's going on, let him have it. Agree on a time to come back together—five minutes, after he's taken a short walk in the fresh air, tonight after dinner, tomorrow after breakfast. A little time can really clear the mind, especially the male mind.

Give your spouse the gift of margin . . . margins of time.

• *Don't use the bed as a weapon.* God never intended couples to use sex as a weapon but rather only for mutual fulfillment (1 Corinthians 7:3–5). Keep your arguments out of the bedroom. The bedroom is a place for unity and intimacy, not hashing out differences.

• *Never, never use the D word to whip the other person in line.* Sometimes tough love is necessary, but when trying to solve normal conflict between relatively healthy couples, threatening divorce will only hurt. It's like taking out a gun and laying it on the table. Comments like these will only validate that you have given up and are not willing to fight for your marriage. Threatening divorce will only cause your spouse to trust you less than he or she already does. "Why keep trying if they are not committed to this marriage?" Threatening divorce is a last resort that should be kept locked away except in extreme cases of ongoing adultery, addictive, or abusive behavior.[2]

• *Contract to control anger no matter what occurs in the conversation or what the other partner says or does.* You can't control your spouse's reaction; you can only control your own. Write out a contract to control anger while discussing difficult situations and sign it, if that helps you both to honor your promise.

• *Agree to call time-out if you sense you or your partner is becoming angry.* If one of you in the course of the conversation overheats, it's futile to try to solve the problem. When your body goes into fight-or-flight mode, adrenaline pumps into your system, blood leaves your brain (which explains why we say and do stupid things), your hair stands up on the back of your neck, your sweat glands pour, your skin becomes oily. You are in a physical state where you are ready to defend yourself. You can't reason or be really rationale.

Agree to walk away.

But come back! Come back to the issue later and start over maybe in a half hour or so.

Wives, it is important for you to understand that though you "are revved up and ready" to address the issue again, men may need a little time to settle down. That's the way he's made. When your husband returns from processing a little, be understanding and cordial; don't attack or belittle him for asking for more time or walking away. And men, do come back. Don't just say you will, do it. Don't allow the time away to become days. If you don't come back to the issue, you make the problem even bigger, adding an issue of trust. Keep your word no matter how much you hate to bring up the original problem again.

> It takes a great deal of restraint and self-discipline to keep your mouth shut when it keeps flopping open, but in order to effectively deal with tough issues, you must learn to exercise smart control during conflict.

Chapter Ten

"A Crisis Means We're Over"

"I didn't marry you because you were perfect. I didn't
even marry you because I loved you. I married you
because you gave me a promise. That promise made
up for your faults. And the promise I gave you made
up for mine. Two imperfect people got married and it
was the promise that made the marriage. And when
our children were growing up, it wasn't a house that
protected them; and it wasn't our love that protected
them—it was that promise."

Thornton Wilder[1]

I SAW HER COMING.

I was walking out the double doors to my office as I noticed Mendi
running toward those doors. She was running a million miles an hour
with a broken heart.

Before I could get to her, Mendi fell onto the sidewalk. Her keys and
purse skidded across the cement. I ran to help. After catching her breath
Mendi screamed out, "Todd has been cheating on me! Todd has been
cheating on me!" over and over. Todd, her husband, was a successful
engineer in our city, and he and Mendi were members of our church.

In that moment, my heart broke for her—and for the kids, and for the marriage. I thought about how it would affect the church, Todd's career, our circle of friends, and even how our children interacted.

I knew this was bad, really bad.

After helping settle Mendi down, getting food and water in her, and calling for someone to drive her home, I immediately called Todd on his cell. "Todd, this is Mitch. What in the world is going on?"

"Don't leave," Todd said. "I'm on my way over there."

After arriving, Todd began to explain what had happened. He had been working with a coworker on a project in Chicago, and during the course of the project, they slept together. Todd said he didn't plan for this to happen, but . . .

After returning home his guilt led him to confess to Mendi that he had had a one-night stand. She reacted as any betrayed spouse would—fiercely.

I knew that there was some stuff going on in Todd and Mendi's marriage, but I never imagined that something like this would happen.

Todd recounted to me some of the things that had occurred in their marriage. About five months prior to the affair, Todd had said something to Mendi about her weight, and she felt so betrayed that she stopped sleeping with him.

Todd knew he was vulnerable, but he started talking to his coworker about how tough things were with Mendi. He said the relationship happened so innocently. He was hoping that she could give some insight into how to help Mendi from a woman's perspective.

The coworker, as it happened, was also going through a tough time in her marriage. Before either of them realized the pit they were sliding into, sparks flew between them. One night after a seminar they were attending and several glasses of wine, they wound up in bed together. Two hurting people medicating their pain.

Over the next five months, things at home were very tense. Todd and Mendi barely looked at each other and stopped talking except when necessary to care for the kids.

Todd told me that he didn't know how to get beyond the hurt he had caused Mendi. Likewise, Mendi didn't understand how to deal with the deep anger and resentment she felt toward Todd. It hadn't been her intention to withdraw further from her husband, but that's exactly what she was doing.

"I DOUBT IT WILL HELP"

We discussed what their options were. I told them I believed strongly that their marriage could be saved. I prayed with them and tried to instill hope at every opportunity. Even when things didn't look too hopeful, I kept preaching hope.

But I knew we were too close to be completely objective. We encouraged Todd and Mendi to work with a licensed therapist whom I recommended. The therapist advised them to attend an intensive conference for couples in crisis, scheduled the next weekend in Atlanta. Like most couples in similar scenarios, they made typical excuses about not going: "We can't afford it. The time isn't best for us."

When they told me about the opportunity to attend, I said, "No excuses! You guys are in trouble in your marriage. You *are* in crisis. As your friend and brother in Christ, I'm not going to stand by and let you destroy a good marriage when something could be done about it."

"But I doubt it will help," Mendi said. "I think this is a waste of time and money."

"Look, guys," I said. "Your children are two of the strongest reasons to go the extra mile in saving your marriage, no matter how you feel. Let's take divorce off the table. It's not the answer here. Your hearts are open to finding a solution—they're just weary. Divorce will only create problems for you. Your children will never get over divorce and will grow up without their mom and dad together in their home because you thought that the way out of pain was to let your marriage die.

"Though you don't feel your marriage can get better, it can. You can save this marriage. I *know* you can. You just need the tools and a new dose of optimism to help get you there."

We prayed together again to ask for the Lord's help and direction.

They finally agreed to go to the conference. But Mendi had a parting shot. "If this doesn't work, I can't keep going on like this any longer. This has to work."

Todd agreed. This was it.

Our friends attended the seminar the following weekend. Fortunately, my prayers were answered and my faith became reality. A miracle occurred for this young couple. They returned from the seminar with a stronger glimmer of hope in their eyes.

In fact, Mendi called me in the middle of the seminar, and said, "As bad as I hurt, I'm beginning to think that maybe we can do this. I don't understand everything yet, but something is happening and I think it may be good."

The Tuesday after returning from the intensive seminar, they dropped by my office. Surprisingly, they were sitting reasonably close to each other—not like newlyweds but close enough to notice. I knew that something different had happened for them. I could see it in their eyes and hear it in their voices. In the past, they had rarely demonstrated any kind of affection in public. It was mostly contempt. But the seminar had clearly helped to break through some walls they had built, and was beginning to help them turn their marriage in a positive direction.

Mendi was the first to speak up after sitting down. "Well, Mitch," she said, wiping tears away, "you were right. There is hope for us. I feel kind of like a patient who has had a heart attack. We almost died, but we were resuscitated." She went on to share how the conference had opened their eyes: "We had really bought into some crazy ideas about each other and our marriage. But this past weekend, a mirror was held up in front of us, and we saw that we were stuck in the same destructive, dysfunctional ruts our parents were. We became the couple we vowed we never would become. The truth smacked us between the eyes. We saw ourselves as we really were and were challenged to look at things in ways we had never before."

She told of a young wife whose husband had had an affair with the counselor at their church. "We saw how even they were willing to save their marriage. We saw them make incredible progress during the weekend. Then at one point we began to think that maybe, just maybe, if they can do this, we can certainly try."

Todd, a true Southern boy, added with a deep drawl, "Yeah, I was ready to shoot this animal and let it die!"

I interrupted and asked, "Do you mean Mendi or the marriage?"

We laughed as Todd continued. "One of the main experiences for me was that I realized that I felt just like Mendi. I was ready to get out. I knew something was really wrong, I just didn't know what to do about it. I was tired of all the arguing and bickering. We had both become mean, hurtful, bitter, and pessimistic people, just like our parents.

"In my screwed-up mind, I began to think that I could confide in another woman and that I would be strong enough to not get messed up. I let my defenses down and let my common sense go out the window. I hurt Mendi deeply.

"I deserve to lose her because of my stupidity, but I don't want that. I want to fight for her. I forgot about all the good inside her. I stopped seeing the beautiful woman I fell in love with years ago. I even convinced myself that I really never loved her in the first place. That was a lie. I know it was.

"Now, I see things differently. I realize that we really are the same people we were when we fell in love. We just don't think or act like them anymore. I am willing to try whatever it takes. I am 100 percent committed. There is a chance for us to make it, after all."

There is nothing more beautiful and fresh than renewed hope.

Todd and Mendi continued weekly counseling. They began to work on the principles they had learned at the intensive. After a few weeks of ongoing prayer, and sincere efforts to transform attitudes and behaviors, they began to think, feel, and act better toward each other. Todd and Mendi began to be attracted to each other once again. Todd worked every day to prove to Mendi that he could be trusted. They started to work out together at the YMCA and got back into shape. They began to think and behave in ways similar to when they first fell in love.

They did not allow themselves to buy into the destructive myth that "a crisis means we're over."

LEARNING FROM CAIN

As with Mendi and Todd, you may find yourself in a season of your marriage where you're experiencing deep pain . . . perhaps a time when you feel alone, rejected, overlooked, neglected, and desperate as to what to do. Satan isn't helping, either. Remember, he has his fingers in this situation on both sides—yours and your spouse. God, on the other side, feels your pain deeply. He knows you hurt. He is exceedingly concerned.

Remember the story of Cain and Abel in the Old Testament? When Cain wanted to kill his brother, Abel, something he knew very well was wrong, something he knew he couldn't get away with, God took time from His busy schedule to come down from heaven and to talk to Cain.

Although Cain knew what he was about to do was evil, he was in such an emotional stupor, in so much pain, so deceived by the Enemy that he moved forward to go against everything he knew as right.

The core issue for Cain was his jealousy. God had showed favor on Abel's offering above his offering. The Scripture says, "So Cain was very angry, and his face was downcast" (Genesis 4:5). Apparently, so was his attitude. His thinking was leading him straight to destruction. He was heading down a murderous path.

God reasoned with Cain as a concerned father would reason with his distressed child, "[Cain], why are you angry? Why is your face downcast?" (Genesis 4:6). Basically, God was saying, "Why is your thinking in the gutter Cain? What are you thinking about that is leading you down such a dark road?"

God went on to say to Cain, "If you do what is right, will you not be accepted?" (Genesis 4:7). In other words: "Cain, think about this, don't you know that if you only do the right thing then the right results will come? You feel rejected now, I know that. But don't you know that I am a just and caring Father, and that if you will only make the right decision, then I will accept you and embrace you? Make the decision in your heart (thinking) to do the right thing, then the right behavior will follow, and the right emotions will come—acceptance, approval, and satisfaction."

But then God took His pleading a step further. "If you do not do what is right, sin is crouching at your door; it desires to have you, but you must master it" (Genesis 4:7).

How powerful this statement is! It sends chills up my spine.

God is clearly saying to Cain, "Control your sinful thinking. Master it. Get it under control, now! You must do it. If you don't, if you delay, if you hang on to this poison in your heart, Satan will walk through the door that he is knocking on. Don't do it, Cain. Don't let him in. It isn't worth it!"

You know the rest of the story. Cain opened the door that Satan so persistently knocked on.

Like any hurt father, God immediately asked, "What have you done? Listen! Your brother's blood cries out to me from the ground" (Genesis 4:10). Abel's blood was the sound of life that has been ended. It was the sound of extinguished opportunity. Opportunity to work this out with an only brother. Opportunity to work together as a team.

This story reminds us that Satan preys on weakened souls. Satan wants to convince you that you should do whatever you want, to follow your emotions, to find yourself. He encourages you to live for yourself for a change. He tells you, "A crisis in your marriage means it's over," and he presents the strongest case he can.

But God is also knocking on the door of your heart.

He comes down from heaven to talk to you as a Father. He reminds you that your feelings can be wrong. He encourages you to look at the truth, to look beyond what you want, what you feel, and what seems to be in your best interest. He calls attention to the fact that Satan lurks in the bushes, ready to maximize the harm if you allow him to.

Maybe you are thinking the grass may be greener on the other side of that marriage fence. It looks greener. It feels greener. It smells greener. And why is it so green? *Because you are watering it with your mythical thinking.*

You may be thinking that ditching this marriage will give you an opportunity to start over . . . that you will find someone who will treat you the way you ought to be treated . . . that the same problems you experience now will not be in the next marriage.

But after years of working with many couples who have remarried, I can tell you that the "starting over" option rarely leads to anything but increased pain. I often observe the same problems, habits, and dysfunction being carried from one marriage to next.

Yes, there are exceptions. The couples who have successful second marriages are the couples who deal with the negative issues of the first marriage successfully.

THROUGH THE STORM

People in crisis often have a difficult time differentiating between the way things *are* and the way things *seem* to be—what is truth versus what your emotions keep screaming at you. You feel that things are hopeless, that there's nothing that can change the situation.

But think of a thunderstorm. Even during the darkest, most terrifying moment of the storm, there is still hope. The sun is still shining above those swirling clouds with the same intensity as it always does. But when you're in the heart of the storm, you can't see it. It's hard to even believe in a blue sky or the sun's golden warmth. The clouds conceal any rays of hope. Your focus is on what is occurring at that very moment—the danger, darkness, and destruction of the storm, not the light from the sun.

If you keep driving long enough during the storm, you will eventually get through it. The wind will calm, the thunder and lightning will temper, and the dark clouds will begin to diminish. Suddenly, the sun will burst through the clouds again, just as bright as ever. You then realize that everything is going to be okay. The initial crisis is almost over.

But there will still be aftereffects, won't there?

Having grown up on the Gulf Coast, I was always told that most people aren't killed in a hurricane; they don't meet their demise from the gale-force winds. Most storm victims lose their lives trying to negotiate the aftereffects. This includes flooding, electrical shock by downed power lines, and cleanup accidents.

When we're going through storms—or picking up the pieces after the crisis has passed—we need someone to say, "You know what, it's going to be okay. It truly is. The sun is still there and it's going to break through any time now. You will get better. You're not going insane. God still cares and so do I."

Isn't that what God does for each of us? He walks beside us and guides us through the storm. The Shepherd Psalm, Psalm 23 illustrates this so clearly:

> Even though I walk through the valley
> of the shadow of death,
> I will fear no evil, for you are with me;
> your rod and staff, they comfort me. (verse 4)

When passing through a valley, our ability to see the light of day is often obstructed by the towering mountains on each side of us. When we walk through the dark valley of tribulation and trial, our ability to see God clearly is also impaired. It is during these times that we need to remember that these trials are only temporary and will pass.

Don't be afraid of the darkness. It is through darkness that God can show His children true light. It is in darkness that God does His greatest work. After all, in the beginning when He created this magnificent universe and world, He created them out of complete darkness and void. *Shadows and darkness are no challenge to God.* That is why we should depend on Him the most when we are facing a storm. What looks dismal to most people is an opportunity of growth and development to God.

Remember that every marriage experiences problems. No matter how long you have been married—one year or forty—you will have problems. That's just an axiom of life. People who say they have never had problems, never had so much as a ripple on the glassy surface of their marriage lake, just don't have credibility with me.

Besides that, it sounds boring.

So, just because you have difficulties communicating, or have disagreements over key issues, that doesn't mean you need extensive professional counseling.

Couples have been working through problems in their marriages—beginning with Adam and Eve—for thousands of years. Couples can solve most problems on their own. The more they mature and the more success they gain in managing problems, the better they become.

God created us with the ability to manage our marriages in a healthy, successful way. Problems are normal. It's okay to have problems. Just because you do doesn't mean your marriage is doomed. Couples today need to learn, develop, and commit themselves to solving and managing problems and crises in their marriages.

Just because your mom and dad divorced and possibly friends and coworkers also divorced, that doesn't mean you will or should.

Problems can actually be very positive in the overall strength and health of marriage. Difficulties and challenges can cause couples to grow deep roots that are able to survive and handle the worst of storms.

HOW DO YOU KNOW WHEN YOU NEED HELP?

All couples have problems. Some are pretty serious, others are minor. How do you determine which call for outside help?

What must be determined first is whether this problem has developed beyond normal to abnormal. In other words, if your problems have become unmanageable and unhealthy and are causing extreme distress emotionally, physically, or spiritually, you may need outside, objective help.

Seek outside help if one or both of you recognizes that the marriage is beginning to develop unhealthy patterns of conflict, communication, or if one or both of you begins to withdraw from the marriage.

Seek outside help if resentment begins to take up residence in your marriage. You need to address the root problems and not simply react to the surface issues (what appear to be the problem). For example, you may feel that your spouse doesn't care about you, but the core issue may be that you said or did something that deeply hurt your spouse. Or the presenting problem may be finances—"We can't control our money." In reality, the core problem may be that you don't communicate about money in a healthy manner.

Other indicators are that you need professional help are family and friends. If they notice that your marriage is out of control, you should heed their notice. Often family and friends can see your problems in a different light than you can. Emotion takes away objectivity.

An often overlooked indicator of the need for outside help is the behavior of your children. Children are pretty accurate barometers of marital health. You and your spouse may have accepted current inter-actions as okay, but your children—even very young ones—can nor-mally sense that something isn't right.

Children, teens especially, often "act out" your marital tensions. It is common for them to respond to tension in their parents' relationship by getting involved in something that's out of character for them.

Another very practical, commonsense indication that you need help is when you find that you've stopped doing some of the loving, healthy things you once did. If you used to like each other, laugh with each other, spend time with one another, serve each other, communicate and solve basic problems together, but now you don't do any of these things, you do have a problem, and you probably need some help.

My experience has been that while one spouse may be ready to get help and move forward, the other may have bought into the myth "A crisis means we're over." Others may simply be resistant to get help. Maybe your husband thinks that everything is okay. Or that the two of you can solve the problem on your own. You have begged, pleaded, and cried, but nothing seems to work.

For over fifteen years, I have been using a plan I developed to help a spouse who is approaching his or her mate about getting help for their marriage. Here are a couple things to remember:

• *Consider timing.* Don't just throw the need for getting help on the table anytime. Make sure your timing is right. Don't bring up the issue of getting help if either of you are going through a stressful time. If your wife has had a stressful day, it's probably not a good time. If the boss just told your husband that there may be a layoff soon, the time may not be right. If the kids have maxed out your nerves, save the suggestion for another day. Before you broach the issue of seeking outside help, make sure it's not a time of high stress and conflict.

• *Watch your tone.* If you bring the issue up with an angry, sarcastic, accusatory, or condescending "parent-to-child" tone, you will probably get the same tone in return. Loud, angry, bitter tones will only cause your spouse to shut down or run. Try dealing with the issue from a different angle.

• *Try a different way of communicating.* If your spouse gets defensive or irate every time you bring up the issue of getting help, maybe you should use a different form of communication. When anxiety or sensitivity is high, I have found that writing a letter may be most effective. At first this may sound a little elementary or simple, but writing difficult thoughts can come across better sometimes than speaking them. Plus, when you write a letter, you have time to really think about what you are saying. You can double-check that you are saying exactly what you intend to say. Rather than being face-to-face, the "space" and think-time a letter provides the reader can be valuable. Writing a letter provides a buffer against instantaneous reaction, which often comes with direct communication of a sensitive subject.

• *Don't attack.* Whether you write a letter or talk directly, don't approach the issue of getting help with the "you need help, I don't" routine. Realize that you both have a problem. If it's a marriage problem, it's an "us" problem versus a "you" or "me" problem. Use a concerned approach versus a blaming one. Let your spouse know that you are concerned that if the two of you allow the problem to go the way it is, it will only go downhill. Raise the topic with no finger-pointing or bringing up examples of how messed up you think your spouse is.

• *Deal with the elephant in the room.* Don't keep avoiding the issue. At some point, say something like, "I know you are uncomfortable with going to a counselor. So am I. But I also know it's uncomfortable for both of us to try to keep living like this."

• *Do your homework.* Find out as much as possible about the person you are recommending to see. Give this person a call and ask for any information that may be helpful in making your spouse more comfortable in coming to see him or her. Come up with several names in case your spouse is resistant to the first one you present.

• *Consider other options.* If you are not yet in a crisis but your spouse is resistant to counseling and the issue seems to be closed, ask him or her if there is someone that you both would consider a mentor? Do you know an older couple at church who may be willing to help? Do you have friends who have gone through similar issues in their marriage? What about your pastor? Is he trained to help, or does he have experience in helping couples in your situation? Is there a Christian seminar like Family Life or Love and Respect[2] that you and your spouse could attend? Often a seminar or retreat—or even reading a book together—will open a door for positive changes in your marriage.

• *Consider intensives.* Intensives are three-to-five-day group sessions specifically engineered for couples in crisis. A crisis is typically defined in this context as "one or both wants to leave the marriage." Intensives are typically led by trained, licensed therapists. Intensives have an impressive success rate (around 90 percent) in turning around troubled marriages, even marriages where deep trust issues such as infidelity have occurred.

Intensives treat couples in crisis as if they are in crisis. They go quickly to the issue and provide insight, practical steps to take to turn things around, and a group experience that can't be duplicated in a traditional counseling setting.[3]

• *Pray.* Prayer can open hearts when nothing else can. When you call on the Father with a humble heart, your prayers can unleash possibilities never seen before. I have seen marriages "prayed" back together when the success could not be counted to anything else. God can heal when no man can: "Is any one of you in trouble? He should pray. . . . The prayer of a righteous man is powerful and effective" (James 5:13, 16).

You may not feel very righteous right now, which is okay. The best of God's people struggled in their faith and fell short. Elijah wasn't perfect and didn't always respond perfectly (1 Kings 19:1–5), yet the Bible tells us: "Elijah was a man just like us. He prayed earnestly that it would not rain, and it did not rain on the land for three and a half years. Again he prayed, and the heavens gave rain, and the earth produced crops" (James 5:17–18).

When you need a reprieve from the rain and storms in your marriage, prayer can bring relief when nothing else can. When your marriage is dying from drought, pray for rain. Ask God to send what you need. He will. He is faithful.

There is help available. Sometimes the difficult task is to reach out and grab the life ring.

A crisis does not mean your marriage is over. That is a myth, plain and simple. No matter what it takes, no matter what you are going through, your marriage can be turned around.

STEPS TOWARD HEALING

Based on my own experience in working with couples in a crisis, I have developed a model that I use on a regular basis. It is neither foolproof nor flawless . . . but it does work. It's my way of reminding couples that "a crisis DOES NOT mean we're over."

I do not claim originality for these principles; I have simply added my own experience and knowledge to others' models in order to develop a practical and effective model of intervention.

This particular model is not necessarily applicable for couples who have addicted partners (addictions to alcohol, pornography, unhealthy relationships, etc.). The example I provide here applies primarily to couples who are experiencing a marriage that has lost its zest and seems to be going downhill. This is prompted by the type of crisis that typically occurs when an unusual amount of stress or unresolved conflict causes the level of anxiety to become too intense for the couple to manage. As a result, anger, resentment, dissatisfaction, complete frustration, and hopelessness take control of the relationship. The couple typically continues the negative engagement and interactions or disengages completely from one another and the relationship shuts down.

This is what I refer to as the *boiling point* or *marital meltdown* in the marriage. It is usually at this place in the crisis process that a couple calls, seeking help from a counselor, a minister, a friend, or a family member.

Here are a few steps I recommend.

1. *Start.* No matter what your spouse does or doesn't do, you start the process. It may be as simple as deciding to not respond to your spouse's attacks. Or it may be as big as calling a counselor to set up an appointment. The first step is always the most difficult. In order to make it to the bottom of a hill, a car must start down the hill. In order to make your marriage better, someone has to begin the process. That someone is probably you.

2. *Commit yourself to do "whatever it takes" to work through the problem at hand.* This includes attending an intensive, a weekend intervention retreat, short-term counseling/marriage intervention, and communication enrichment seminars. Additional helps could include long-term counseling, reading books, working through workbooks together, scheduled time together, homework counseling assignments, and having regular date nights. Conduct online research to discover what resources are available in your local area (workshops, classes, seminars, etc.). Try to gain a similar commitment from your spouse. But if you can't at this point, don't worry. This is a normal situation. It is rare for both spouses to be equally committed at this point.

3. *Establish mutually agreed upon rules of interaction.* These are behavior boundaries that will help reduce friction and tension. For example: (1) no finger-pointing, (2) no screaming and shouting, (3) no blaming, (4) no "you" statements—only "I" statements, (5) no continuing of habits that infuriate and inflame the other partner, (6) no using the kids as message mediums, (7) no sabotaging each other's advances, (8) no

overindulgence of hobbies (television, computer, shopping), (9) no negative body language (frowns, rolling eyes, heavy sighing, silent treatment), and (10) no withdrawal of affection.

4. *Cut off outside relationships that may hamper the healing process.* If a friend, family member (including extended family), or coworker's involvement seems to be causing friction in your marriage, back off from that particular relationship. The risk of hurting that person's feelings should be less of a concern to you than the possibility of causing additional damage in your marriage.

If one of you has been having an affair, you must completely terminate all interaction with the affair partner. Terminate, not simply suspend. This means no phone calls, no e-mails, no explanations, no parting last words, no apologies to the affair partner!

Healing and reconciliation cannot occur as long as there is any type of ongoing interaction with the other person. This is not optional. There are no loopholes. Cutting off outside relationships also includes friends at work and chat-room acquaintances. A good rule of thumb is this: It is best to suspend or discontinue any outside relationship that could have any possible negative affects on your marriage. No relationship should be more important than the relationship with your spouse!

5. *Teach and model healthy communication and conflict resolution.* Here is a wise saying that makes a lot of sense: "If you do what you have always done, you will get the same result." This is so true of communication and resolving conflict. If the present style of communication has brought you to where you are (in a mess), the present style must not be very effective.

You and your partner must be willing to swallow your pride and accept that you are both communicating poorly. Each of you must use a great amount of restraint and discipline to make necessary changes. Each of you must learn to control your mouth. Making unnecessary statements to your partner only produces huge gaps between you and your mate. Just because you think you have a "right" to say something doesn't mean that it's worth the damage and separation it may cause in your relationship in the long run.

Unhealthy conflict management causes relational sprains, bruises, and broken hearts. Following the steps I've suggested or attending workshops and reading books on communication and conflict resolution may feel like wasted time when you're in the midst of a stressful season in your relationship. The adversary of your soul (and your marriage) will whisper that all your efforts will only amount to rearranging deck chairs on the *Titanic*.

But that's just one more marriage myth from the "Father of Lies."

The truth is, you can learn some specific steps to resolve conflict in your marriage. Even baby steps count!

In the New Testament book of Romans, in the space of just a few verses, the apostle Paul speaks of "the God who gives endurance and encouragement" and "the God of hope" (Romans 15:5, 13).

Endurance . . . the power to hold on and keep believing.
Encouragement . . . fresh courage to square your shoulders and move forward into a new day.
Hope . . . a settled confidence that the God who loves you and your spouse will work night and day on your behalf as you trust in Him.

With help like that from God, with the wind of heaven at your back, you can keep climbing the upward path toward healing and renewed love.

One step at a time.

Chapter Eleven

"All Pain in Our Marriage Is Bad"

When written in Chinese, the word "crisis" is
composed of two characters—one represents
danger and the other represents opportunity.

—John F. Kennedy[1]

WE HAVE A LITTLE WIENER DOG named Flash. He is the greatest dog in the world. Currently he is living with relatives in Mississippi. I guess he's in the process of being adopted. My father-in-law says we will have to kill him first to get Flash back. I thought about it . . . but decided Flash isn't that special. (But we still have his papers in case he wants to come home.)

As great as Flash is, he has his bad points. He doesn't like snow. He is built so low to the ground that the snow really bothered the sensitive parts of his little body. When he lived in Colorado, he even learned to walk through the snow with his hind legs hiked up in the air. Poor fellow.

So, we sent him to a warmer, subtropical climate, which he enjoys immensely. The only problem is that our in-laws spoil him. He gets hamburgers, fried catfish, and peanut butter sandwiches. The last time we saw him, he had "really filled out." He's a little chunk. He couldn't walk on his front legs now if his life depended on it.

Flash is the most gentle, sweet dog you will ever find. He's like an old man—placid and unhurried. Flash loves kids. Under normal circumstances he would never bite anyone. But one day when Flash still lived with us, a friend of ours came to visit with his ten-year-old grandson who had recently been adopted from Russia. The little boy and Flash got along very well, until Daniel accidentally put his knee down on Flash's paw. Flash bit him on the nose.

We felt terrible. Rhonda went to the ER with them. Eight stitches. We called the parents and apologized. We kept waiting for the "you are going to be sued letter" to arrive in the mail, but it never did. It really wasn't our fault, and it wasn't really Flash's fault. It was the *Flash principle* that caused him to bite.

Under normal circumstances most healthy people will act normally. But if they are in a great deal of pain, they may act totally different. Pain has a way of overriding everything we know to be right, moral, and good.

"THIS IS BART IN PAIN"

Through the years I have witnessed the kindest of people, the strongest Christians in the world, curse, hit, yell, threaten simply because they were in deep emotional or physical pain. Bart, for example, was the kindest, most devout Christian in the world, but when he received the call that his wife, Teresa, had been found dead from a heart attack in her cube at work, he reacted under the influence of grief. He cried, screamed, and cursed. He put his fist through the wall. He broke dishes in his home. He turned over tables and sofas.

"This isn't like Bart," a friend said.

"Yeah," I responded. "Well—this is Bart in a lot of pain."

Pain really does have a way of overriding normal emotions, behavior, and responses. If your spouse is going through a tough time at work, a health crisis, or a family issue, then more than likely he or she will probably act in ways that are not characteristic. A quiet, reserved husband can transform into a strong, assertive protector if he or his family have been wronged. A wife who is normally an outgoing social butterfly can withdraw and become extremely depressed during a crisis.

Couples need to understand this principle and try to be as supportive and helpful as possible when one or both goes through a tough time. Struggles are often like hurricanes. After they rumble through, most things change dramatically.

If, however, after a difficult period, you or your spouse seems to lock into an ongoing unhealthy pattern, such as depression or anger, then you probably need to see a licensed therapist or a medical doctor.

A word of advice—don't EVER underestimate what your spouse may be going through when he or she is sick and dealing with emotional or physical pain. No matter how insignificant the problems may seem to you, it is real to your spouse. He or she needs to know that you are there, supporting—not judging—and praying. It doesn't matter if it is life-threatening or not. All pain is real and takes a lot out of you. It is so easy to become insensitive to the pain others experience.

A few years ago I was reminded about how difficult it is to experience pain. I was taken to the emergency room experiencing some of the most excruciating hurt I have ever experienced in my life. As I paced the floor and rolled in the ER bed for several hours, the doctor told me I had three medium-sized kidney stones.

The pain was incredible.

There is really nothing you can do to get out of the pain from a kidney stone; once it starts, it doesn't let up. You must simply ride it out and suffer.

After the intense pain lingered for several hours, I began to feel sorry for myself and begged God, the nurse, the janitor, people in Europe, anybody, to please help me! I watched the clock and it seemed to be in slow motion.

The experience gave me a renewed admiration for those who suffer with ongoing emotional or physical pain. It also reminded me how important it is to be surrounded by caring people when walking the grueling road of pain. When you are in pain, you need someone there to hold your hand, wipe your brow, or simply stand by your side.

When it comes to marriage you must constantly be aware that when your spouse is in pain, biological or emotional, he or she does not think or respond normally. To expect normal behavior in such circumstances borders on cruelty.

You should be conscious and alert to any of your own actions or thoughts that may impede or make your spouse's struggle worse. You must be willing to err on the side of being too sensitive or doing too much rather than making the mistake of not showing that you care.

It's easy for people to forgive mistakes you might make while they are hurting, if you respond with sensitivity and compassion. However, if you fail to respond in any way because you underestimate how much impact the struggle is having on your spouse, then he or she will likely have a difficult time overlooking your negligence. Always err on the side of compassion.

Nobody orders a plate of pain. There's no demand for home delivery when it comes to unrelenting hurt. Pain is never easy to experience. Everyone, including you and your spouse, wishes to be out of pain.

THE GIFT OF STRUGGLE

Just because you are struggling with something painful in marriage, or even if you have been struggling for years, you still must believe in the value of staying in the process. You may struggle because of deep, painful emotions and experiences, but don't short-circuit the process by trying to remove yourself from the pain.

You may think that your pain is too great to bear . . . but it's probably not. You may think you can't get through another day . . . but most likely, you can. You may tell yourself that you've reached your limit . . . but most of us have "limits" well beyond what we tell ourselves.

(If, however, you are being abused, that is something totally different. Put this book down and get to safety. Call someone who can help you.)

There have been numerous times in my own marriage, especially the early years, when I thought, *This is it! There is no way I can live with this any longer.* But I did. And I'm eternally glad that I did.

It is often the tiny, insignificant annoyances that build into mountains we can't see over. So, we start looking for an exit sign. Don't do it! Don't jettison the journey of a lifetime—you have no idea how beautiful the vistas may be just a few miles down the road.

Don't shortcut the struggle.

Don't remove the larvae from the cocoon.

Don't take away the irritating grain of sand from the oyster.

If you do, you will never see the butterfly soar or the pearl glisten.

In Psalm 103, David describes God as a tender father who loves His child with a special kind of love—*lovingkindness*. In Hebrew, the word means "kindness that has been added to." This psalm paints a picture of a God who remembers us like a merciful father showing pity to his little child. "Lovingkindness" conveys the image of bending the knee to help someone in need—like a father who kneels down to show compassion and mercy like only a loving father can because his child has scraped her knee.

My friend, that's the way God loves us. He hurts when we hurt. This does not mean He will pull us out of the ring when we get beat up and bruised. He knows that in order to win we have to stay in the ring, pain and all.

No good dad will pull his child out of the soccer game simply because he or she misses a goal or gets a rough kick in the shin—unless they are in danger. All good fathers realize that pain is part of the process of growing up.

Life is sacred. It is a gift. It should never be taken lightly or for granted. It is too frail and can be snatched away in a breathless moment. Every one of us is a heartbeat, breath, or car length away from death. Life is designed to prepare and shape us for eternity. That's why you and I have no right to take it . . . not by abortion, and not by suicide. Life is not ours to take; that rests in the hands of the Creator.

Marriage, like life, is also sacred. It is a gift. We hungered for it in our youth. We signed on the dotted line. We asked God to give us a good spouse. And He did. Your spouse is still the same good-hearted person you married years ago, maybe just a little more bruised up.

Marriage is part of God's plan to make us fit for eternal living. We do not have a right to withdraw from it, abandoning it emotionally or physically, just because we feel like it.

Don't be afraid of the process. Don't be afraid to fail. Failure and sin are the very things that distinguish us from God. If we never failed, we would not need a God or Savior. It is because of failure and sin that we have access to grace. We would never know the euphoria and ecstasy of grace if we didn't fail.

The psalmist wrote:

LORD, if you kept a record of our sins,
who, O Lord, could ever survive?
But you offer forgiveness,
that we might learn to fear you.

I am counting on the LORD;
yes, I am counting on him.
I have put my hope in his word.
(Psalm 130:3–5 NLT)

We would never know what it really means to love and be loved if we didn't fail. So, when your marriage seems hard and struggles appear around every corner, don't let yourself believe the myth that "struggles mean we're doomed."

Struggle is a gift.

Chapter Twelve

"Marriage Is Just Too Hard"

Someone once asked, "Is there anything more
beautiful in life than a young couple clasping hands
and pure hearts in the path of marriage? Can there be
anything more beautiful than young love?"

And the answer is given, "Yes, there is a more
beautiful thing. It is the spectacle of an old man and an
old woman finishing their journey together on that
path. Their hands are gnarled, but still clasped; their
faces are seamed, but still radiant; their hearts are
physically bowed and tired, but still strong with love
and devotion for one another. Yes, there is a more
beautiful thing than young love. Old love."[1]

TODAY ONE OF THE MAJOR MYTHS that frightens many dating couples—and perhaps even those of us already on the journey—is the delusion that marriage is just too hard. That it is almost this "once attainable, gone-with-past-generations fairy tale."

That's a lie (yet another one), straight from Liar Number One.

Marriage is as good an idea today as it was in the beginning. It still works. It still blesses. It's still the best thing going in a sometimes lonely, mostly cynical world. There's a good reason for that. Matrimony has survived and spanned thousands of years since Adam and Eve, because it came from the heart and mind of God.

The Bible opens the history of mankind in the context of marriage. It closes by inviting us to the marriage between the Lamb and His bride (the church). The Bible uses the analogy and sacred institute of marriage to teach us some of the universe's most important messages in life.

It was in the context of marriage that God taught us how families can survive sin and tragedy in the story of Cain and Abel. It was in the context of marriage, through the story of Hosea and Gomer, that God taught us how to forgive—even when our loved one has been unfaithful. It was in the context of marriage that our Lord was born and brought up, raised to be the Savior of the world. Ananias and Sapphira taught us the painful truth that husbands and wives can make decisions, even together, that can be deadly. Priscilla and Aquila taught us that we can serve together and make a difference in our world.

I don't think that God would abandon something as important as the institution of marriage just because many of us today aren't perceiving it, cherishing it, or staying committed to it. Don't you agree? Our mishandling and failures do not determine the value or future need for something as sacred as marriage.

Sometimes, the answer to lost satisfaction, managing conflict, adjusting attitudes, restoring lost intimacy, and revitalizing a dull sex life is "showing up"—recommitting, getting back to the basics in marriage. Don't let yourself succumb to the myth that "marriage is too hard."

SMALL INVESTMENTS, BIG DIVIDENDS

The thing about old clichés is that some of them have been repeated endlessly through the years because they contain enduring truth. But maybe some of those truths need a fresh spin, or a new perspective.

Take that old saying your grandmother used to tell you: "You need to save up for a rainy day." Well, there's wisdom in that, but I'd like to take it beyond the piggy bank or your passbook account at the bank. In the context of our discussion in these pages, I would urge you to make small, consistent investments in your marriage. In other words, commit yourself to relationship banking.

That's a concept that's been around for a while, and I can understand why. It's a simple but effective analogy.

Relationship banking simply says that you must put deposits each day into your spouse's account. The more deposits you make, the better off your marriage will be. No matter how skilled you are and how much the two of you love each other, it's inevitable that withdrawals will occur from time to time. Withdrawals are anything negative that causes a spouse hurt or negative feelings.

In real-life banking, what happens when you make more withdrawals than deposits? Overdraft. The same is true for your marriage. If you make more withdrawals than deposits, your relationship will become bankrupt.

When you were dating, you probably spent as much as thirty hours a week together. Because of that amount of time, you put multiple deposits in each other's account. This built closeness and trust. You felt like this person you were dating was the queen or king of the world, and you treated him or her accordingly.

During the first couple of years of marriage, you likely continued to add more deposits than withdrawals. But nothing in life is static. Because of stressors, hurt, resentment, and misunderstandings, you are now making fewer deposits and more withdrawals. The economy in your marriage has gotten way out of balance. Things are not as good as before. If you aren't careful, you'll go into the red. Your marriage will become bankrupt.

Something has to change. You must go back to the basics.

Start putting deposits back in your spouse's account no matter whether he or she understands, accepts it, or even reciprocates. No matter how your spouse treats you, do it anyway. Remember, in your vows you said, "For better or for worse."

As I mentioned earlier, serving each other can turn a marriage around in a heartbeat.

What are some ways to put deposits in your spouse's account?

1. *Cut down on the withdrawals.* If you know which actions or attitudes constitute withdrawals for your spouse, then stop these immediately. If you aren't certain what they are, ask your spouse to list two or three withdrawals on a piece of paper, and then offer suggestions on ways you can stop the withdrawals.

2. *Perform random acts of kindness.* Think of something that you have done for your spouse in the past—something that made him or her feel good. Do it again and surprise your spouse.

   Think of something you may have intended to do but have not yet done. If you are the guy, make sure the action does not have sexual attachments. Consider offering your wife a night alone with the girls or a gift certificate for one to a local restaurant. Or gals, offer your husband a coupon for a round of golf, sex on a night other than the designated times, or take his car to have it washed. Notes, cards, and kind and flattering words go a long way also. These are all simple ways to make deposits in your spouse's account.

3. *Don't expect return deposits.* That's not the idea. Maybe those reciprocal deposits will come, and maybe they won't. You can't focus on that, and you shouldn't be keeping an account. If all you can think about is giving to get, then you really haven't engaged in giving at all. Besides, your expectations may far exceed what your spouse is capable of at that point in the process. Sure, you can suggest deposits . . . but don't over-anticipate. Don't let yourself become hurt or resentful if they fall below your desires. Simply embrace and celebrate the deposits as they come and continue to make daily deposits in your spouse's account.

4. *Be sure to acknowledge your spouse's investments.* If your husband or wife has taken the time and thought to make a direct deposit in your marriage account, be aware of it. Let your mate know how much the action or word meant to you. Really praise your spouse and reinforce the behavior so it will likely occur again. Men, especially, are like puppies, so reinforce the behaviors you want them to repeat.

5. *Realize that withdrawals are a reality*! No one can be around another human being for very long without making a withdrawal. Learn to accept the fact that your spouse is human and will make mistakes. Some little, and some not so little. Don't question his or her integrity simply because he or she drew down their account. Don't blow the situation out of proportion. Learn to choose your battles. Ask, "Is this something that's really worth the energy to respond to?" and "Can I live with this mistake, especially in light of the fact that my spouse just made a deposit an hour ago?" Give each other permission to make occasional withdrawals, but commit to making at least three deposits for every withdrawal and watch your marriage become healthy and vibrant again.[2]

WALKING YOUR WAY TO A BETTER MARRIAGE

Many times, simple solutions are best—even something as simple as walking together.

This is a practical way to solve problems and feel more connected to each other without feeling you have to have a PhD in marriage. Many couples—even those who have tried marriage conferences and waded through the ocean of marriage information today—can feel overwhelmed at times, or confused about how to strengthen their marriage.

It's easy to max out on information in this "information age" in which we live. Sometimes, instead of reading another Internet article or watching another marriage DVD, the best thing to do is simply take your spouse by the hand and take a walk in the fresh air.

You can often achieve emotional, physical, and spiritual intimacy in a marriage by simple practices, such as walking together, writing letters, taking evening drives, praying together, or completing a service project together.

Whatever schedule you decide on, once a week, twice a week, or every day, walking time also creates talking time. Life will cause you to forget matters you need to talk about, but if you have a structured time together each week, you will likely remember to bring things up. In our hectic world, if you don't plan time together, it won't happen. Protect your walking time as you would your work schedule. It's that important.

Walking provides a nonthreatening forum for men because they don't have to make eye contact. Men tend to say more and open up more when they are walking. Especially at night.

Rhonda and I seem to think better when we're walking together. We have solved a world of family, marriage, financial, and spiritual problems in our walking shoes. Walking gives us an opportunity to discuss kid issues, in-law issues, church issues, career issues, and on and on it goes. It's a way God has used to strengthen and restore our marriage during times of misunderstanding. We have worn out several pairs of walking shoes together.

Isn't it amazing how God uses simple, basic things to do big things? That's His style. He used a young shepherd and five stones to win a war. He used a bunch of regular people walking around a city to bring it down. God uses the simple things in life to forge the most important things.

And next to your relationship with God, your marriage is the most important aspect of your whole life.

WRITING—AND RIDING

Here are several other "simple" ways to deepen your relationship.

• *Write.* Putting pen to paper (okay, most of us now find a computer more comfortable) allows you to say things you wouldn't or can't express face-to-face. It is also a great avenue to express difficult issues and to ensure that what you are saying is actually what you intended to say. It even gives the listener time to absorb what you are trying to say without pressure to immediately respond. Writing can also crack open a closed heart and allow the goodness inside to pour out. Don't buy a card with somebody else's predigested sentiments. Say it yourself, in your own words.

Letter writing should not be the only means of communication between you. Nor should writing be used as a weapon to say things to hurt the other because you don't have the courage to say it to his or her face. That's malicious. And this method certainly isn't to be used to accuse, attack, or employ unfair, exaggerated language such as "You always . . . " or "You never . . ." Stay away from using accusatory pronouns and stick with, "This is the way I feel . . ."

Writing is a simple way to communicate and bond when you can't do it any other way. Remember, God's Word, His letter to us, is the main channel He chose to connect and communicate with us. Writing is a great way to communicate our love to the other.

• *Hold hands and give hugs frequently.* Touching each other stimulates the release of oxytocin in the body. Oxytocin is the bonding, cuddling chemical that creates feelings of intimacy and closeness.[3] It's the same chemical that is released when a mother nurses her baby. The more you and your spouse touch, hold hands, and sit together, the more oxytocin you will both experience. Try sitting on the couch together and holding hands or walking to the car holding hands.

• *Take rides together.* We bought a 1989 Saab convertible for $2,500. It was the best investment we have made in our marriage in years. We get out regularly in the Colorado mountains and just drive. Sometimes we talk. Sometimes we simply ride. We call it our marriage car. We hold hands, talk, and connect. It was worth the money—ten times over.

SEVEN UPS TO A GREAT MARRIAGE

One of the neatest marriage ceremonies I have ever performed was on a pier extending out into Pensacola Bay in northwest Florida. The weather was perfect. As a gentle, tropical breeze rippled in off the water and the sun sank into a calm, blue sea, this young couple vowed their hearts to each other.

I'd met Jerry and Beth Anne at church. Jerry was a soda delivery driver who delivered 7Up, Pepsi, and other refreshments to our church building. I had the chance to get to know Jerry by hanging around the vending machine each Thursday afternoon around three. We struck up a great friendship. Before long the young couple was coming to church regularly.

Not only did I have the opportunity to take them through premarriage counseling, but I also had the chance to share the gospel with them. One week before I married them, I baptized them. What a great opportunity.

I racked my brain to come up with a unique, but simple ceremony for this fun-loving couple. But this is what I came up with: "Seven Ups to a Great Marriage." Jerry and Beth Anne loved it.

So as we close the last chapter of this book and end our conversation together, I want to leave you with these words of encouragement that I shared with Jerry and Beth Anne on their wedding day. Don't let yourself ever believe that you and your spouse won't make it, that marriage is just too hard. Marriage is well worth the effort. Just ask Jerry and Beth Anne.

1. *Light up.* To keep the fire going, every time one of you walks into the room, let your face light up in delight. Send the message throughout your years together that you are delighted to be in the other's presence (Song of Songs 2:14; Proverbs 15:13).

2. *Dress up.* Don't allow yourselves to get sloppy. Stay physically fit. Present the best you have to your spouse. Sure you can relax, but don't allow relaxing to become an excuse for living in a state of carelessness. Take a bath or a shower. Put on some makeup.

3. *Stand up.* Become each other's strongest supporter and advocate. Don't ever speak negatively of the other to friends, coworkers, or family. Assume the best about each other. Trust each other until you have solid reasons for not trusting, and even then, learn to trust again. Stand by each other's side when times are good and when they're not, when it's the popular

thing to do and when it's not. Stand by your spouse when no one else will. Believe the best about each other when it would be easy not to (1 Corinthians 13:5 –7).

4. *Start up.* Start each day with prayer and time alone. Couples who begin their day praying together will have an edge on the competition—more strength, better attitudes, and clearer perspectives about the challenges of the day. Prayer frames the day and its events in a heavenly perspective. Couples who do this are taking God along in their journey together that day. There's no better companion.

5. *Shut up.* Learn when to speak and when to be quiet (James 1:19). Count to ten before responding to something hurtful the other says. Learn when to walk away and when to walk back together (Proverbs 10:19; 12:18; 16:24). Let your words ring with tones that are sweet to the soul. The tone you use may be just as important as the words you use.

6. *Pull up.* When the other becomes discouraged, you should become his or her greatest cheerleader. Become a broker of hope in your marriage. When emotions, experiences, and life say it's not worth it, you assure your spouse it is. Find at least one thing that you can encourage each other about every day. This investment will pay off a thousandfold (1 Thessalonians 5:11; Hebrews 3:13).

7. *Look up.* Don't depend on your own strength to make your marriage successful. Look to the God who made the sea, sky, and mountains. If He can fashion such wonders, He can also create wonders within you. When you don't know what to do or say, remember, God does. Ask Him. Some days you will not feel like being kind and serving each other, but because you serve the Lord, you will do it any way—"as to the Lord" (Ephesians 5:22).

When you have tried everything you know to do, when you've read every marriage book you can get your hands on and you're still struggling, God is probably calling you to look up. When you look up, God will provide insight and strength you can't get anywhere else (Proverbs 3:5–6; Philippians 4:13).

My prayer is that these Seven-Up principles will refresh your marriage from weariness, boredom, and loss of direction.

I also pray that you will be able to change your thinking—to expose some of the myths we talked about. Myths are so deceiving. They seem so right, so natural. You may have heard them repeated over and over. But a lie is still a lie, no matter how many times it's told, and myths in marriage can cause a great deal of havoc.

Don't try to correct every myth, every invalid thought, in one afternoon. Work on one at a time. Take baby steps toward a better marriage. If you mess up and make a mistake, don't give up.

Keep on dancing.

You can't waltz if you don't keep trying.

Notes

.

CHAPTER TWO: "ATTITUDES DON'T REALLY COUNT"

1. Yogi Berra, *The Yogi Book: I Really Didn't Say Everything I Said* (New York: Workman, 1998), 123.

2. Lisa Dutton, "The Power of Positive Thinking: Easing Depression," McGill University Health Centre, February 2003.

3. For more information about Focus on the Family, see their website (http://www.family.org) or write to them at: Focus on the Family, Colorado Springs, CO 80995.

4. Bob Brooke, "Oregon Trail: Wagon Tracks West," *HistoryNet.com*. http://www.historynet.com/oregon-trail-wagon-tracks-west.htm.

5. W. E. Vines, *A Comprehensive Dictionary of the Original Greek Words with Precise Meanings for English Readers* (McLean, VA: MacDonald, ND), 572.

CHAPTER THREE: "I NEED TO CHANGE MY SPOUSE"

1. For an in-depth look at the four "animal" personalities, see the book *The Two Sides of Love* by Gary Smalley and John Trent (Colorado Springs: Living Books, 2005).

   To take the Marriage Insights Personality Inventory, go to: http://www.leadingfrom yourstrengths.com. While there download the free *Marriage Insights Workbook*.

CHAPTER FOUR: "I DIDN'T MARRY MY SOUL MATE"

1. "Napoleon Dynamite (2004) Memorable Quotes," *The Internet Movie Database*, http://www.imdb.com/title/tt0374900/quotes.

2. John Gottman, *Marriage Clinic: A Scientifically Based Marital Therapy* (New York: W. W. Norton, 2000), 22–23.

3. Linda J. Waite, Don Browning, William J. Doherty, Maggie Gallagher, Ye Luo, and Scott M. Stanley, "Does Divorce Make People Happy? Findings from a Study of Unhappy Marriages," *AmericanValues.org*, http://www.americanvalues.org/html/does_divorce_make_people_happy.html.

4. Ibid.

CHAPTER FIVE: "MY NEEDS COME FIRST"

1. Diane Sollee, "Marriage Quotes," Smart Marriages: The Coalition for Marriage, Family and Couples Education, http://www.smartmarriages.com/marriage.quotes.html.

2. Dr. Bill Doherty, *Take Back Your Marriage: Sticking Together in a World That Pulls Us Apart* (New York: Guilliford, 2003), 14.

3. S. M. Stanley, S. W. Whitton, S. M. Low, M. L. Clements, and H. J. Markman, "Sacrifice as a Predictor of Marital Outcomes," *Family Process* 45 (2006): 289–303.

4. Doherty, *Take Back Your Marriage*, 36.

5. Ibid., 38–39.

6. David Popenoe, "The Future of Marriage in America," *The National Marriage Project*, Rutgers University, July 2007, http://marriage.rutgers.edu/Publications/SOOU/TEXTSOOU 2007.htm.

CHAPTER SIX: "HAPPINESS IS EVERYTHING"

1. Jone Johnson Lewis, "Happiness Quotes," http://www.wisdomquotes.com/cat_ happiness.html.

2. "Researchers: Marriage Doesn't Make You Happy," CNN.com, http://www.cnn.com/ 2003/HEALTH/03/17/marriage.poll.reut/index.html.

CHAPTER EIGHT: "I SHOULDN'T HAVE TO ASK"

1. Bob Phillips, *Phillips' Book of Great Thoughts & Funny Sayings* (Wheaton: Tyndale, 1993), 333.

CHAPTER NINE: "CONFLICT IS BAD"

1. John Gottman, *Seven Principles for Making Marriage Work* (London: The Orion Publishing Group, 2004), 24–27.

2. For more on the topic of tough love, read *Love Must Be Tough: New Hope for Marriages in Crisis* by Dr. James Dobson (Carol Stream, IL: Tyndale, 2007).

CHAPTER TEN: "A CRISIS MEANS WE'RE OVER"

1. Diane Sollee, "Marriage Quotes," (from the play *The Skin of Our Teeth* by Thornton Wilder), Smart Marriages: The Coalition for Marriage, Family and Couples Education, http://www.smartmarriages.com/marriage.quotes.html.

2. Learn more about Family Life at http://www.familylife.com, and Love and Respect at http://www.loveandrespect.com.

3. For more information on intensives for couples in crisis, go to my website www.mitch templeonline.com.

CHAPTER ELEVEN: "ALL PAIN IN OUR MARRIAGE IS BAD"

1. John F. Kennedy, "Address to the United Negro College Fund Convocation" (Indianapolis, Indiana, 12 April 1959), as quoted in *The International Thesaurus of Quotations*. Rhonda Thomas Tripp (New York: Thomas Y. Crowell, 1970), 123.

CHAPTER TWELVE: "MARRIAGE IS JUST TOO HARD"

1. Diane Sollee, "Marriage Quotes," Smart Marriages: The Coalition for Marriage, Family and Couples Education, http://www.smartmarriages.com/marriage.quotes.html.

2. For additional reading on the Love Bank concept, see *Love Busters* (Grand Rapids: Revell, 2007) and *His Needs/Her Needs* (Baker, 2001), both by Dr. William Harley.

3. T. R. Insel, "Oxytocin: A Neuropeptide for Affiliation: Evidence from Behavioral, Receptive, Autoradiographic and Comparative Studies," *Psychoneuroendocrinology* 1 (1992): 17.

DR. GARY CHAPMAN ON THE MARRIAGE YOU'VE ALWAYS WANTED

Many blissful couples often uncover some jarring realities: a trail of dirty socks on the floor, conflicting opinions on how much money to spend on shampoo, and more. Beloved relationship expert and marriage counselor Gary Chapman offers his trademark practical wisdom on the many issues young married couples face.

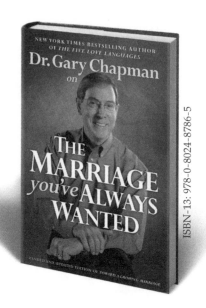

ISBN-13: 978-0-8024-8786-5

THE FIVE LOVE LANGUAGES

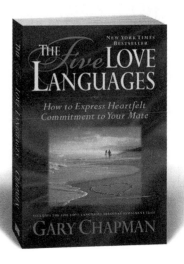

ISBN-13: 978-1-881273-15-8

Dr. Gary Chapman explores the all-important languages of love, helping each partner discover which actions are interpreted by the other as loving and affirming, and which as indifferent and demeaning.

Comes with study guide.

MOODY
PUBLISHERS.
1-800-678-8812 · MOODYPUBLISHERS.COM

LOVE TALKS FOR COUPLES &
MORE LOVE TALKS FOR COUPLES

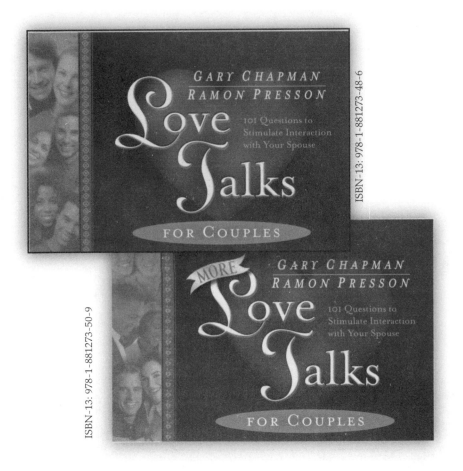

Your spouse is a fascinating person with meaningful, humorous, and profound experiences, feelings, ideas, memories, dreams, and convictions. These questions celebrate the depth and wonderful mystery of your mate. Questions invite disclosure, and disclosure launches discovery. Discovery enriches a marriage and builds intimacy.

1-800-678-8812 · MOODYPUBLISHERS.COM

THE 10 COMMANDMENTS
OF MARRIAGE

ISBN-13: 978-0-8024-3145-5

In words that are profound, often humorous, but always biblical, Ed Young draws from decades of counseling couples to provide ten commandments for a lifelong marriage that sizzles. God wants your marriage to be nothing short of incredible. And it could all begin with this amazing book

1-800-678-8812 · MOODYPUBLISHERS.COM

THE MARRIAGE PRAYER

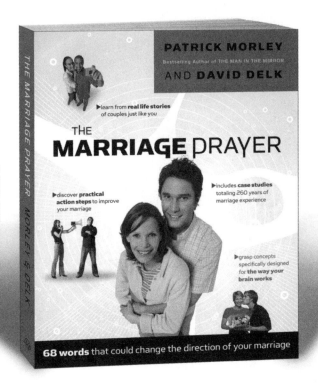

Marriage is the most significant human relationship we ever experience. Yet many people do not think about how a great marriage happens, and why. Designed to enhance learning and promote communication, *The Marriage Prayer* covers key topics ranging from worship and security to money and sex. Filled with case studies, application questions, and real-life stories, this book will keep you moving down the road toward a godly marriage.

MOODY
PUBLISHERS.

1-800-678-8812 · MOODYPUBLISHERS.COM